STEALING HOME
A FATHER, A SON, AND THE ROAD TO THE PERFECT GAME
Ron Seybold

Austin
2019

Copyright 2019 by Ron Seybold
All rights reserved.

For permission to reproduce selections from this book, contact Permissions, Skin Horse Press, 11702 Buckingham Road, Austin, Texas 78759

Visit our website at skinhorsepress.com

Publisher's Cataloging-In-Publication Data

Names: Seybold, Ron, author.
Title: Stealing home : a father, a son, and the road to the perfect game / Ron Seybold.
Description: Austin : Skin Horse Press, 2019. | Includes a list of resources and inspirations.
Identifiers: ISBN 9780985006730 | ISBN 9780985006747 (ebook)
Subjects: LCSH: Seybold, Ron--Family. | Fatherhood. | Fathers and sons. | Little League baseball. | Baseball--Miscellanea.
Classification: LCC HQ756 .S49 2019 (print) | LCC HQ756 (ebook) | DDC 306.8742--dc23

Book design by Asya Blue

Printed in the United States of America

For Dot, the stair-mom who backed me up with her play at the plate, so I could swing for my heart's fences.

This all happened. You could look it up, some of it. Some of it is the other kind of history, the sort that comes from storytellers. A few names have been changed, or shrouded, as an attempt at kindness. Memory is a map, drawn by people who were there. The years scuff up the ball, smooth out the dirt on the infield, and make all stories true as remembered. Never argue balls and strikes.

CONTENTS

Introductions
Warm Ups
Opening on the Road
Lost on a Getaway
Joysticks and Sidearms
Concrete Balks
A Break at the Jake
Love on the Point
Minor Key Memory
Storm Warning
Day Game Dad
Wrigley Sunday Service
Praying for Better
A Perfect Team
Home at Last
Acknowledgements
Resources and Inspirations

INTRODUCTIONS

The lights are winking out at Kaufmann Field in Kansas City as I shift in the seat of our rented convertible. I'm trying to find the way out of the parking lot, but my mind isn't firing on all cylinders. Ten hours of driving already from Texas to get my son and me up here on a hot July Saturday night. Then nine innings of even more sitting. Now I have to find the hotel. Sweat collects on the inside of my ball cap as I realize I have no clue where I'm going.

It is not my first time in this parking lot, just my first time here when I wasn't high. Fourteen summers after my night of that Willie Nelson show in KC—one that ended wrestling my sleepless mania as I clutched a kitchen knife, paranoid from too much pot—my 11-year-old son Nicky sits with me in the convertible. This trip is supposed to prove I am not running from my fatherly duty after a divorce and court-managed custody. My summer visitation vacation will be just the two of us, and I have thirteen more nights to take care of him on my own. I am committed to being a better father than my dad was for me. Fatherhood without anger can't be so hard. Not so hard that a man would have to kill himself because he failed at it—like Dad did in the same year I sat in this parking lot for the first time.

The sound of the crowd milling in the lot turns rowdy while the dashboard clock ticks toward midnight. It is 1994, so there is no phone in our car to check for hotel directions. I flip my AAA Triptik pages forward, then back. I squint in the dashboard light at the map's red and black lines. Then I pull out our Rand McNally Baseball Atlas and skim with alarm at the Kansas City Royals entry. These maps are my guardrails for traveling across eleven different states to see nine games in only eleven days. I lower our Pontiac Sunbird's top to study the maps.

"Do you know the way?" Nicky asks.

I assure him, unconvincingly, that I do. I set out to find our hotel in the dark. Conscious of my untreated anxiety issues, I need to locate safety before the pounding in my chest takes over. Nicky believes in me more than I believe in myself. I am driven to be the man he thinks I am.

The July wind helps me take a breath. The lights in the lot lead us to a sign that promises a freeway. The ramp hides in the dark, though, with the glare of the light shining off my glasses and blocking my vision to the left and right. I eke across two streets, stop at a light, then turn left toward the sound of the Interstate.

Just get to I-70, I say to myself, and then we'll be all right.

I drive underneath the Interstate, though, and scan the streets to the left and right. Where is the ramp? I sit up straighter and slow the car. Nicky slides down in the seat as we enter the gritty streets of what I'd have called the ghetto when I was his age. Hooded heads swivel at the two white guys entering the neighborhood in a convertible, cutting through the soundtrack of a Saturday night.

We stop at a light and Nicky knows the biggest mistake first.

"Uh, Dad." He's fading on me.

"Yeah, what?"

"We're in the hood, and wearing bandanas." I'd bought them to keep the sweat out of our eyes during the game. "We might be wearing colors, Dad."

I force a laugh. A real parent wouldn't drive into the worst part of town wearing something that dangerous. A real parent wouldn't bring his son to a street full of drunks and lined with razor wire. My anxious self careens straight into the clutch of dread. My stupidity is going to get us jumped, carjacked, killed. I keep the car moving, not stopping to roll up the top or the windows. I don't even stop at the red light.

As I roll through that light, I see two cops in a patrol car just shake their heads, watching me try to steal the way home for the night with my son.

WARM UPS
Spring, 1994

On a Little League field in April of that same year, I took my first steps toward that summer's journey. I bounced along at a slow trot with Nicky, matching his pace on opening day. In 1994, it was easier to focus while at the ball field, with no cellphones or smart devices to distract us. We warmed up his arm with outfield tosses before his game. I watched him play, and the time during those games was when I loved him and my fatherhood best. The games were my sweet spot with my only child. I was trying to find a path to fatherhood, using only the weekends that the divorce permitted me.

On that day I was ruled by anxiety, a condition that didn't even rank as a disorder in that era. My father had ruled our family through rage, and it was my own choice to repeat his lessons about anger. He was my father when he raged and Dad when he did not. I would give my son a different example to follow. A two-week baseball vacation from the bottom to the top of the country and back was the best way to prove that I was not the same as my father. It was to be an unmedicated trip, a challenge I never examined. Like my own days as a boy, Nicky was just one rage away from being unsafe with his father.

Terms of my custody arrangement restricted me to alternate weekends, a practice that was customary for the time. Less frequent contact would keep me cool, too. Verbal assault had knocked out my first marriage, separating me from Nicky. I left my marriage stricken with shame. Mine became a broken home, using my mom's language, although she took my side in her blindness of solidarity. She had a hard line about the un-broken home we grew up in and what would've happened if she left Dad in a divorce.

"I think if I'd have left your father, we wouldn't be alive today," she told me just before the road trip started. "He would've found a way to burn down the house with us inside." She reported this as casually as a thunderstorm forecast or a warning of a sub-zero winter night.

By 1994 I was four years into a new marriage to a loving woman named Dottie, and I vowed that no moment of anger would stain our marriage or any time with my son. The best way I could feel safe in fatherhood was to play games with Nicky. Sometimes it was basketball, but the solid thump of his ball in my glove at that field on that morning reminded me how easy the games made it for me to show love for him. I had become his part-time, playmate parent. On that opening day for his Little League team, Nicky threw a clean and clear strike to the glove of my heart.

I spied his smile under his blue cap and said, "Ain't it great to be playing in the daytime?" Heaps of rust-red infield dirt sat beyond the outfield. A netted alley for batting practice ran out away from the diamond.

"Yeah, I like day-timers better than the others. They remind me of

Wrigley."

"What do you mean?"

"Day games. You know, at Wrigley. I got to go with Randy last year."

Randy. His stepdad. My counterpart and imaginary rival, although that gentle man had no contest with me. Wrigley. Bleacher seats, Nicky said. The Bums. Classic.

By 1994 the Cubs had played 82 seasons at Wrigley and only the last six had been under the lights. Day-timers there, lots of them. The field in Chicago, so classic that it's nicknamed The Friendly Confines, features outfield walls covered with thick ivy by summertime. Nicky saw it first with Randy, a fine man who nevertheless got his own two exclusive summer weeks with Nicky. I compared, as I always do.

I don't know if Nicky saw a look clouding my face, but what he said next hit home. "I should take you there sometime, Dad. Wrigley's great." I trotted closer to see if he meant it. "Really, we could go together."

"Just us guys," I must have said. I don't remember my steps up to the bleacher plank and my waiting scorebook. I was already planning dreams for our summer on the road. Like a pitcher in a season of pinpoint accuracy, I could control my wild throws of anger. I just got two weeks to prove it to everyone, including me.

WRIGLEY WAS A PLACE OF DAYTIME BASEBALL LEGEND. After my divorce, I learned about playing in night games. Each week included a Wednesday visit to play with Nicky. Before his mother and I split, Nicky used to play me in checkers, Chutes and Ladders, Trouble, and even Pong on our console TV. But in the beginning of my divorced fatherhood, I didn't have any games on hand for us to play. That's how swiftly I left his house in exile.

I would erase all of that with an epic journey toward two perfect days at Wrigley. Those majestic afternoons—not just one, but Saturday plus Sunday—would sweep away my doubts about how special my bond with my boy looked. The rest of my world was judging me. I had an answer for that. Only a great dad would turn over two weeks of his life to his son so they'd see a thick sheaf of baseball games together, riding in a rented convertible all the way. I could do enough parenting to keep everybody safe, marginally clean, and out of jail.

Nothing about travel is guaranteed, though. The inky night hours I spent in manic planning in April and May, before we drove our first mile, sometimes made my heart pound with worry. I always worried because the unexpected was always out there. There was joy out there, too. I knew it. I was sure I could map a route to find it.

I knew nothing of what would enflame my reactions to unforeseen troubles, any delays, or some other shortfall of my manic certainty. A vacation of two weeks with a tween is no test to take without ample study, but I didn't let that hamper me. I wouldn't have let myself drive with Nicky solo across Texas—let alone from the bottom to the top of the country—if I'd been an honest judge of my anxieties.

Anxiety and depression were the roots of my fatherhood failures. I had no interest in any such label of mental disorder as I drove into our vacation. I rode into parenthood with vague intentions to be a dad better than my own. I ran from any possibility I could fail like he flamed out. Dad was churlish, compulsive, and domineering. His black rubber comb swept his hair thick with Vitalis straight back from a widow's peak, a family feature I'd passed along to Nicky. Dad was a chieftain whose gifts were cerebral, his hazel eyes often lit up with the intellect and scrutiny needed to create things. He did not often create words of soft love on those lips under his brusque mustache. It was the Sixties and some men couldn't speak such words easily. I needed his words but did not know how much.

In my generation after those silent Sixties dads, I spoke such words once I became a father. I knew how to act out my part in public, but in that convertible beside my boy I'd be performing in private, just Nicky and me. I had faith I'd speak those loving words even when things might be imperfect. I had to believe in that love and push away the memories of my failures in places like the trailer home where Nicky first grew up.

By the time I planned our summer trip I'd marched into self-employment to erase the rules of my last bad job. Despite my haste in the way I fled the job, I wasn't damaged goods—of that I was certain. Nobody was going to get damaged during our weeks on the road. I peeled away the calendar pages that spring, waiting for my opening day on a fresh season of fatherhood.

For most of Nicky's childhood, I was Custody Dad—that father you'll see ordering in the fast food places on Fridays with his kids or pushing them in supermarket carts on the first, third, and fifth weekends. Custody Dads make the best of what's given. We also get a couple of unbroken weeks with our kids each summer, and I learned to reach for a showy vacation, the kind of melodramatic road trip to make up for everything else I was lacking as a father. Custody weekends started at Friday suppers and lasted until sundown Sundays, short enough to sidestep any conflicts that might get out of hand. I didn't discipline Nicky in my unbroken 48 hours of fatherhood every other week. It was my golden time. On the road, though, somebody would have to keep us on schedule and safe from the unexpected. That would be me over much more than a weekend's worth of parenting. I would have to stretch my patience and control my anxieties for half of July to see nine games and cross nine state lines.

While pumping up the trip, I told myself I'd be savoring my summer's time with Nicky by seeing more ballgames than anyone else could. My secret motivation was to drive enough miles to show Nicky's mom that I could care for him on my own. Dottie would not be with us, unable to buffer any splashes of my anger or my panic in anxious moments. Dottie had two decades of motherhood that I relied on when Nicky visited. I would be parenting without her love as a backstop. I could do this, I reckoned, remembering my best plate appearance on the day Nicky was born.

ON THAT FINAL DAY OF 1982 I TOSSED A PERFECT PITCH OF A STORY. After spending my first few hours as a new dad in a birthing suite, I arrived sleep-deprived and joyous at my sportswriter's keyboard, replaying a moment from my hospital morning. The doctor turned my infant's head during delivery, revealing a miniature of my own face. The echoes of Dad's face were there too, the signature widow's peak of many Seybold men. Sitting at those newspaper keys my hair was still wet and shaving cream lurked behind my ears. Now that Nicky had arrived, my Hill Country News column was overdue.

I glowed while my fingers danced on the keys of the paper's typesetting station. I usually composed on an IBM Selectric, but I was so close to deadline that the typewriter would delay the newspaper even more. I love the manic spotlight. I might have written something different back in my office on the Selectric. Perched under the florescent lights of the composing room, with people waiting and watching, was like performing onstage. After all my words about other boys in my game stories, I finally had my own son to adore like the parents I saw at games. I didn't think that morning. I just wrote, like a pitcher watching the ball all the way up to the catcher's mitt. A pitcher's mastery only arrives when he can stay fully in the moment. Those precious games are usually crafted from a smaller number of pitches. My "Sports Shots" column was under 500 words.

His tiny fingers grip my pinky, and I think of a curveball pitcher. His little legs kick off the blanket, and I picture a football star. His sad cries will fill my house with loud woe, and I hear an avid fan rooting from the bleachers.

He is Nicholas Maximillian Seybold. He is just four hours old today. And he is my son.

Nicky is a little sport who is destined for big things. He burst from the starting blocks with a sprinter's speed and a miler's heart, breaking life's tape at 10:02 AM, already an all-star in my heart.

I stood like a track coach beside the hospital bed as my wife pushed him to life. With a stopwatch for timing contractions dangling from my neck, I remembered what my high school coach used to holler from across the infield as I drove to the finish of the quarter-mile. "Kick, honey, kick!" I heard myself saying, as she bore down and brought him to be.

And now hours later, the wonder of that performance hasn't dulled. I dream of him stealing bases, intercepting passes, racing on the fast break. Today his eyes began to track. Watching those blue-green orbs follow my fingers while I am changing him, I know a tennis title is only time away.

Already he's taught me the meaning of sacrifice. My wife and I will tend to his helpless little body with the care of expert trainers, marveling at a human in miniature. His pain is ours. We soothe his aching cries with the balm of love.

And the compliments will come. "Oh, what big hands," I hear. A backcourt dribbling whiz comes before my eyes. "What big feet," says another admirer in the room. "He'll be a big boy." A leaping free safety jumps in my dreams, stealing a touchdown pass in the end zone.

Today I know the source of the passion of parents in the stands. My pride in my son will outlast any overtime. I'll cheer him on, win or lose, remembering days when I was god-like in his world, amazed at how he's grown from them.

If he doesn't play, he may cheer. I look with longing to afternoons when we'll share third-base seats and hot dogs at a summertime doubleheader. For I want my son to know—to live is to play, to compete is to improve, to try out is to grow.

But most importantly, Nicky will learn he was born onto a team of people as big as his heart, and love will make him a winner every time. Today I'm a proud co-captain. My blue-chip off the old block has scored big in my heart. Today MVP stands for My Valuable Person, a little guy who'll bring me championship seasons the rest of my days.

It was the first thing I wrote that drew acclamation. In the weeks that followed, people would call to report a score, or hear me on the phone asking questions and tell me how wonderful that writing sounded. How happy they were for my plainspoken joy about fatherhood. The column was overloaded with sentiment, but the words were a stew that those parents wanted to swallow in gulps.

Best of all, I'd written something brief enough to meet the sportswriter's goal, a tiny gem. In the opening week of my second full year married to Nicky's mom, I believed I'd fixed my anger of Year One. That sports poem to my boy was supposed to be proof. I wasn't a mad man like Dad. I'd been reborn as a father of kindness. That was the role I believed I was born to play. The ballpark road trip was supposed to be a revival of that show of kindness.

OPENING ON THE ROAD
Rangers vs. Blue Jays
The Ballpark in Arlington, Arlington, Texas
Friday, July 15

Over-packing our vacation schedule was an old practice of mine. Attending nine games in eight different cities in five states would take planning, an itch I scratched with compulsion. Baseball's season schedules are tightly woven like a high-class business suit. In 1994 the 28 teams were to play 81 home games each in ballparks from San Diego to Boston and Miami to Seattle. That full season was scheduled to be 2,268 games. Right from the start of that year there were serious threats of a strike, though, a worry that could ruin our tour by erasing games.

The *Sporting News 1994 Baseball Guide*, thick with schedules and rosters, gave me data that the Internet would provide years later. I mapped out possible game days with *Street and Smith's Baseball Guide*, cross-checking with the *Rand McNally Baseball Atlas* open across my desk. The atlas was a marvel with three full-color pages for each team, crowded with maps and seating charts and hotels. I drove the trip over and over in my head, trying to plan out the perfect route to maximize our time together.

Nicky helped us find our way. He inked all our potential stops on a calendar from his mom's Jewish temple. Inside each date's box under the Jewish Year 5754 in July, he listed the games available at every ballpark within three days drive of Austin. I gave him those calendar parameters and a list of all the available cities, which he scrawled in red-lettered abbreviations—DET-KC or STL-NYM. I started to imagine the trip as a two-week Fatherhood Series. Everything felt more real when it had a nickname like that, like something I'd dream up for a column.

Limits make life more genuine than perfect, though. The atlas was great for mapping the way to ballparks, but the calendar would rule where we could see games. I carved out an itinerary on pages of legal pads, crossed out and rewritten. Perfect planning, perfect trip. I rewrote our schedule in ink because it looked assured.

I am my father's son, so the cost of anything has always been crucial. I can display a few skills of a quant, the kind of calculating genius that lets me track the time of day without a clock nearby, or write headlines that fit neatly within a single newspaper column. I drew up totals for our hotel nights, the $1.15 a gallon gas across more than 3,400 miles, the car rental, our 18 tickets. I took a deep breath. Although the cost was high, I intended to spend even more. We'd drive in a rented convertible, because the family Toyota Tercel was not special enough. That aged econo-box probably wouldn't survive the trip, either. This perfect trip demanded a Pontiac Sunbird convertible where I could hear Nicky call me "Dad" while we headed for each new ballpark and fresh hotel. The rental was extra steep because the car company charged by the mile, too. As a freelance writer, I didn't have any vacation cash saved, so I'd use my credit cards for two straight weeks. Maybe I'd return emotionally richer, though, bearing real proof of my parental skills and my son's love.

Our closest park heading northward to Wrigley was the Rangers' new stadium three hours away in Arlington. I never doubted it would be our first game. The next closest park within a day's drive onward to the Great Lakes was in Kansas City. We'd cut through eight states to get to my boyhood hometown of Toledo and a game up in Detroit, then turn west toward Wrigley in Chicago. The perfect weekend was those day games in Wrigley between Nicky's Cubs and my boyhood favorites, the Cincinnati Reds.

I'd have to drive for two weeks with no relief to get us there and back. I made dozens of phone calls while I planned and then called back to confirm what I'd planned. There was no other way in 1994. It was a time without the Web, Wi-Fi, or phones that rang in our pockets. Long distance was billed by the minute, paper tickets were sent to the mailbox at my curb, and hotels could only arrange for rooms through phone calls. People used travel agents. I offered up every manic minute of planning as proof I loved him. I could not leave anything to chance like tickets. Only poor planners had to buy scalped seats, I reckoned.

Whenever I talked with Nicky after days of not seeing him, our safe talk was about sports. Baseball became our glue by 1994, alongside a thicket of memorized dialogue from the *Simpsons* episodes, lines we traded back and forth as if they were baseball cards. I would tape the shows on Sundays after he'd left, so we could rewatch together on his weeknight visit. "I had no idea a father could be so important to a child's behavior," Homer would say, a line we'd repeat with snickers. Unsure what to say to my son at times, I'd fall back on TV's smartest comedy.

As Nicky grew old enough for Little League, though, I taught him the loud language of baseball. You can holler at a game on TV and nobody gets scared. At a ballpark people also yell. In Little League, fathers are supposed to be nice. Usually nobody takes offense.

BY OUR TRIP'S OPENING DAY NICKY WAS DEVELOPING a passion for music as deep as his love of baseball. Dottie's son, a Gen-X hipster of 22, introduced him to the Red Hot Chili Peppers, Stone Temple Pilots, and other titans of '90s rock. Music could fill our silences during all those miles. We toted a four-pound case of 44 CDs. A CD player was rare in any car rental, though, so I channeled my dad's engineering skills to rig up a portable Discman that fed music into our convertible's cassette player.

A better car would have a built-in CD, I thought to myself. It's okay, it matters more to you than to Nicky. Or Nick, as he was starting to ask to be called. Approaching his teenage years, Nicky wore his sawdust-blond hair long and tousled. Shampoo your hair, pick up your room—those were all somebody else's commands. Custody Dad is a non-authority figure. I played the good cop to his mom's bad. I wondered about the times I'd need to enforce discipline over our two weeks.

I overcompensated as Custody Dad, renting the sky blue Sunbird sporting a white top, fierce air conditioner and cruise control. The radio was loud enough to pump songs above any whipping Interstate winds. The Sunbird was not as cool as 1994's convertible darling, the Miata. But because of rental agreements, the Sunbird was the only convertible I could rent to cross so many state lines. Rules of the rental road were another detail I had to resolve over the phone.

When we picked up the car, Nicky heard me tell the fellow at the Enterprise counter I was thrilled to be driving a rag-top. My son slouched beside me while the clerk rang up the rental. Nicky whispered, "Rag-top. Why?"

"The top's made of cloth."

"It's not ragged, is it?"

"Just a nickname."

"You and your nicknames."

Here was a moment the Simpsons could smooth over. Rag-top was like Simpsons milkshakes. They're not just milkshakes, I explained, when the Simpsons talk about them. "Let's take the boy for frosty milkshakes," I said in my best Homer impression.

"The boy?" he echoed to me at the counter. "You mean there really is a Bart?" He was The Boy. I was Homer and loved him, sometimes clumsy but always with passion. The *Simpsons* was call and answer for my fathering days. We probably sounded as daft as a pair of asylum inmates on the lam, quoting a cartoon show back at each other, making a mash-up of lines from separate episodes.

I scrawled out my signature at the rental counter to take responsibility for the Sunbird, overlooking any anxiety about vacation breakdowns. Our schedule was so tight that something as simple as a blown fuse under the dash would have struck an entire city from our trip. I had no idea where the Sunbird's fuses were, much less where to look in a parts store for a replacement. I counted on luck to carry us from state to state in a car with a mysterious repair history and a top fancy enough to fold back with a motor.

Dad would not have approved of my carefree moment. My father taught many things, his lessons often arriving on the wings of watching for the worst to happen. Blown fuses were his strong suit; the mystery of repairing one in a thunderstorm was among his most heroic moments. But fuses, whether in a convertible or a suburban bungalow, were not sentimental lessons.

I had no useful knowledge of auto repair to share with Nicky. I was a former sports editor, a job that made me want to teach Nicky baseball as soon as possible. The sport is timeless, or seemed so in 1994, even though designated hitters were still so controversial that half the teams in the majors didn't use them. Baseball unfolds at a pace that makes room for conversation. The game action is there to grease the time, always at hand to comment upon or praise. It would provide that diversion some fathers need with their sons, a meditative act that smooths out the conversations.

I would use our talks to point at details that remain the same everywhere: going into second base high to erase the double-play, or what a catcher does with a face mask when a pop fly floats directly overhead. I wanted to take Nicky someplace to talk about how a second baseman can pretend to throw a ball to first to freeze the runner on the move, then throw behind the base runner to start a rundown. How bare-handing a ball at third while catching a bunt, then uncorking a sidearm toss to first, was a risky move but might be the only way to nail a speedy bunter. How an outfielder's jump on the ball gives a clue about the chance for a clean catch. Chin music, suicide squeeze, basket catch—they were all lessons. Those would be moments of baseball in one city after another. Nine games of them would ensure hours of analysis, insights about something, anything other than my own life so far as a dad.

I DID NOT SUSPECT THAT IN LONG HOURS OF OUR TRIP, so much of it quiet, I would circle some acts of anger in my starter marriage to Nicky's mom. Our tragedy was probably destined, since we met while she directed me in a melodrama. I played the villain and adored the attention. I reprised the part inside our single-wide trailer home.

My ex-wife practiced love as if it were a performance, in public and before any audience. She had icons at hand, the elements we'd made together. Baby. Dreams of owning more than we had. A children's play that she wrote that was produced on a local stage. At one point she was running a day care business out of that trailer home. She added the certainty she was entitled to the best, a trait that we shared. In the roles which our parents showed us, I would be onstage, but not in a supporting part.

"You're just too unhappy for us," she'd say when I'd rant, taking up her regular shield of holding Nicky.

"This isn't just about me. It can't be. You're wrong, too."

"But not angry, like you."

"You don't know angry. My father was truly angry."

"It looks like you learned a lot from him. I should have left you years ago, like I said before Nicky was born." On that afternoon I'd wept on her belly where our baby was growing, begging her to stay.

Like a melodrama, there was a crisis in every challenge I faced—like the rampant shoulder-high Johnson weeds in our front yard, or the mobile home company that sold us a $15 set of rebar and wood-plank stairs for our trailer's front door, then gave us nothing off the back. In the kitchen of our trailer sat a fridge of new vintage, parked hard beside the hallway. The path led past a changing bathroom we stacked with cotton diapers from the service, then onward into a back bedroom where Nicky slept on the rare nights he wasn't in our bed. It was a 14x70 trailer in all.

Few things were precious in that home, but I zealously guarded my one tool of the trade. I had a small portable cassette recorder, a middling Radio Shack CTR-101 I used for my work as a reporter. It was a black plastic wonder no bigger than an airport paperback. Using it evoked happier times with my dad, him busy with his array of tech tools and toys in a basement workshop. The memory from that basement room was buried in my soul. There was yelling in there, though, along with the random joy.

One fiery day I cooked up a calamity from a piece of black plastic gone missing. Nicky had taken the recorder's battery cover off. His curiosity made the tool into a toy. I discovered him playing with the recorder and started shouting at him.

"Nicky! That's not a toy!"

His head snapped up and his small brown eyes, the ones usually full of joy, went wide. I was hurling loud sounds, flashing another entry into his definition of daddy's anger. I can't recall for certain, but in my memory I see him shrink back, somehow being smaller than even a two-year-old can be, sitting on that faux-tile floor and playing with my tool.

"Put that down! Now!"

I didn't say this in a calm voice, or even as a request. I barked a command while trying to shout down my own fears. Had he ruined my tool?

His mom bounded into the kitchen, a room less than a dozen steps away from either end of our trailer. She heard my voice, the anger that sometimes splashed fear onto the two people I loved most. I seized the recorder and examined it, turning it over and over, pressing each button. Everything worked and I calmed down a little.

Then I discovered the battery cover was missing. The two double-As remained in place, but I imagined all the travels my tool would have to make in the weeks and months to come as a sportswriter. I dropped to the floor to search for that cover, maybe hidden among plastic dinosaurs and a Teddy Ruxpin bear at Nicky's feet. It was nowhere to be seen, and my relief gave way to more fear. The anger boiled up in me, like it does. I was having an episode, approaching something manic.

"Where is it?" His eyes blinked at me, his gaze frozen. "I said, where did you put it?"

He had made only a sentence or two so far in his life and knew a few small words. But he couldn't answer. Fright bottled up whatever he might say.

I stomped and screamed. Right into his face. The trailer was too small to let the sound of my voice bounce anywhere but onto my son. My wife stepped between me and him, a mother bear protecting our cub.

"You'll find it," she said. "But you need to calm down."

"You calm down," I shot back. I picked up on her fear. I heard the blood pounding in my ears. "He's always into everything," I howled.

"He's just a little boy. He's your little boy. You're scaring him."

I hurled a chair out of the kitchen and glared as it banged up against the too-thin paneling, gouging the cheap wood. She swooped down to snatch

Nicky off the floor as he started to wail. Once more, a daddy Seybold had scared another generation of boy.

My wife pulled away and I chased after her. She ran outside and held him while he cried. I never wanted Nicky to cower, fearing me later like I did my father. But like a pitcher throwing wild, I had lost control.

I found the cover behind the refrigerator. I cannot be sure how I found calm that day. But my shame arrived swiftly, like it usually does, a stinging cold rain of self-loathing that dowses my flames of anger.

On July 15 Nicky and I posed for the victorious photos that Dottie snapped in the driveway at the start of our trip. My face was flushed with bravado as well as the mid-afternoon heat. Dottie waved goodbye and wished us well.

After she told me she loved me, she added, "Good luck." We kissed and parted for two weeks. Her phrase reminded me my work ahead might be imperfect.

By the dashboard clock it was 90 minutes before the 5 PM Friday rush hour, with the temperature stuck in triple digits. Even though we had the top down, we blew frosty AC around faces that were greased with sunblock and shaded by ball caps. Any man who wasn't trying to show he was a cool dad would've kept that top up to stay cool. Yet I wanted a moment that was perfect, the classic sendoff of a dream. We rolled six blocks away and started to roast, stopped at the trip's first traffic light.

"Gotta keep our top folded down," I told him. I grinned and flexed my hands on the wheel of the rental. I wore a Chinese bandana next to the brim of my cap to keep the sweat out of my eyes. I was trying to stay aware of our first moments, thinking there were another 14 days in front of us, the time where I'd be Nicky's only caretaker. No, he wouldn't need much beyond buying suppers, lunches, and breakfasts, with oh so many at McDonald's. We'd talk baseball to make every mile feel like a pilgrimage, discover ballparks both sacred or brand-new. High mania, high temperatures, high hopes.

"More sunblock, dad?" He held up the Walgreens SPF 30 tube and wagged it. I watched his sweat trickle down from under his Cubs cap, the one he wore during his Little League championship game that year. His hair was a honeyed brown that year, his eyes brown like mine.

"Nah, I'm okay."

He fiddled with the radio. "Can we get the ballgame's station on yet?"

"Not yet. Anyway, they'll be yelling about football up in Dallas." A fresh training camp for the Super Bowl champion Cowboys relegated Rangers baseball to a lesser sport. "We gotta get past Waco, at least."

"Okay." He picked up our grey CD carrier the size of a small-town phone book, two-thirds full of his music and one third mine. He started to leaf through it. "You're gonna like this," he said.

I was ready to like anything we'd play together. "Whatever you want."

That would be my mantra until I didn't have to say it again. I threw the Sunbird into gear and plowed us away from that light and out of Austin. The music bellowed out rebellion, not a theme song for a parent. After 40 minutes of weaving through the racket of diesel exhausts and the roar of the 18-wheelers that flanked the Sunbird, out-barking our stereo, we rolled up our windows while I left the top down. I finally stopped under an overpass to raise our rag-top and turn the AC to the icon that promised freezing.

"Yeah, better," Nicky said. "I can hear my CD now." He pulled off his cap and grabbed one of his R.L. Stine *Goosebumps* books out from under his Game Boy. There would be nothing for him to miss here at Texas mile marker 297.

"We'll put the top down again, later."

"S'okay." He didn't look up. I tried to read him to see if our trip was still fun.

The sun that came through our windows was hammering the cloth top. When I tipped down our visors against the July heat, the silver letters of "Sunbird" slanted the sunlight off the glove box. The windshield was already littered with bugs, too many to wash off with wipers and fluid. In our back seat we carried a bottle of green Windex and a paper towel roll whose edge had been waving in that wind.

"Hey Dad, have you heard this one?"

There was his song to me, that word Dad. I wouldn't have recognized any music of his, but I wanted to connect with my boy. "No, what's it called?"

He held up the CD case in the bright afternoon light. *Purple* by Stone Temple Pilots. He pushed the button on that CD player a half dozen times until the baritone of Scott Weiland rose up. I couldn't follow what Weiland was singing about on "Interstate Love Song," but heroin and a love affair were floating in the lyrics.

The cool of the air conditioner lowered my pulse. We were just driving to a game together, nothing that hard. Just the same kind of trip I welcomed each week, driving to his Little League games where I'd keep the official scorebook. Or down to Dart Bowl for three full games. Or to the neighborhood grade-school playground for some basketball. Sometimes I'd let him win on purpose to fill him with confidence. Our relationship was all about the games.

I was driving into a new era for my family, a time when a father cares for a son in an everyday way, a role my dad rarely played during any trip. Dad got us there and paid our way, carried the metal ice cooler the size of a pirate's chest, and took our pictures. If life is like drawing without an eraser, I didn't know how to draw a picture of parenting beyond that kind of dad. I'd be the guy checking us into motels, lugging a convertible trunk's worth of clothes up and down from each room, looking for the missing t-shirt before we could leave. This being a boys-only trip, all the clothes were wrinkled: a sign of misbehavior. Nicky and I were without any woman's guidance, no one to say, "That's too stained to wear." That missing female voice was not entirely new. There were evenings of just father and son during his visitation when my divorce was still new. We didn't have Dottie on this trip. A woman's heart would be absent for two full weeks, and it was brand-new to both of us.

I shifted into fifth on the Sunbird's stick, the gear I hoped Nicky would think was cool. The basso roar of the engine crept into the cockpit. The car was still free of vacation grime, the signs of riding in it for hours a day, holding snack bags from one exit to the next. The blue cloth bucket seats retained their Pine-Sol scent. We sucked on massive cups of Dr. Pepper and lemonade we bought at the Circle K convenience store in Waco—the last stop I meant to make until the ballpark.

The miles rolled away under the cover of Nicky's tunes from Green Day and mine from The Cars. The guitar solo on "All Mixed Up" gave me a theme song for speed. We might have called our soundtrack a mashup if such a word existed in 1994. The CDs gave us about 500 songs, maybe enough for more than 60 hours of driving.

My anxiety crept closer as we found our way to the ballpark. I stayed out of trouble in Friday evening traffic and tried to conjure up the directions I'd burned into my brain the night before. Thankfully, I had an ally in the seat next to me. Nicky held up the map page from the baseball atlas—maps better than anything AAA gave us in that narrow white plastic bag sitting at my elbow.

"It says 360 North, dad."

"Exit where?" I'd overlooked the sign.

"Right up there. I think you follow those cars."

I weaved across a couple of lanes and held my tongue. I could show him how I'd manage stress, pressing it away into a peaceful look on my face. Nobody would shout inside this car, not like the white station wagon my dad piloted on our trips to Montreal, Virginia, or Sarasota. Here in Texas we wouldn't panic, careening across highway lanes toward an almost-missed exit. No swearing for me. My pact, you know, where Nicky would endure no more anger. I'd be Captain Kangaroo instead, benevolent and wise. The mysteries of fatherhood's rules and discipline were still mine to explore.

Our first night would not be Nicky's inaugural visit at what the Rangers called The Ballpark in Arlington. It was a sparkling new stadium built as a retro park, new construction to mimic old ball fields like Wrigley. The previous year I visited the retro Camden Yards in Baltimore, the first of these new-old parks. The Ballpark game for Nicky would be like our trip to Wrigley: also not his first. I was already two ballparks behind his stepdad. By the time we'd return I'd be five ballparks ahead, though. With me it is always the adding and comparing. I considered myself the home team, always batting last to pull ahead and win.

Nicky's only ballpark trip with me until that day had been to a creaking relic. I once took him to the aged Rangers ball field that this new Ballpark was replacing. We called the old one Turnpike Stadium because it was hard up against Interstate 30 and built out of aluminum like cars. During Ranger rallies there, the crowd would stomp on the metal under the seats and bang the place like a drum. The Ballpark in Arlington would be everything Turnpike Stadium would never be—new and state of art, a poem to baseball as the game once was. It promised a Legends of the Game Museum behind the Home Run Porch. Artifacts like Nolan Ryan jerseys were on loan from

Cooperstown. Ryan had a street named for him in front of the new park.

We carved our way through the city as Nicky called out the streets. Left on Collins. Now a right, coming up on Division. He rattled off the names in a voice bundled with the joy of exploring. He was helping us arrive on time. Then the ballpark of red brick and Texas limestone roared up out of the flatlands all around it. It bore the badges of a retro park, wrapped in classic stone, bounded by shining green railings and gates, built as a monument to baseball's yesterdays.

We entered the ballpark's lower bowl like breaching the doors of a palace. I was so new to fathering in tandem with Nicky's stepdad that I'd mistaken that man for a rival. So my foolish mission was to be more fun than that man. I would make the Rangers' ballpark fresh for my son, somehow.

"Wow." I pointed. "Those skyboxes. Blue, like jewels."

"Like the Rangers' uniforms," Nicky answered.

"That scoreboard out there, so green. Like a hand-operated pine tree."

"Huh?"

"Like pine needles, you know? Same color."

"Oh, yeah, sure. And that grass, it's so—" He paused and narrowed his eyes. "Like an apple, a Granny Smith."

We were playing a game where I knew the field well. Word play. I looked into his brown eyes and then saw the infield dirt over his shoulder. Another mirror of color. But I wanted to toss his phrase back, like the games of catch we'd play.

"Sure, fella, like an apple." Then the Cracker Jack the fans ate was spotted like a spaniel, the oversized hot dogs were pink as any lobster, and so on. Those dogs moved past us, carried in a vendor's box while we stood at the top of the aisle. He watched the food go by. I wanted to show off how well I'd picked seats.

"Find our seats?"

"You bet. But Dad, I'm hungry."

The concourses teemed with places to feed a boy on a vacation. Dogs, fries, nachos. Nothing extraordinary except for the place where we'd eat it. Lunch was hours ago, so I surveyed the menu boards and loaded up.

I carried a tape recorder with me as we walked the concourses. The habits of a reporter are not the best fit for a vacation with a son. Nevertheless

I lurched into another mission, one that would memorialize our vacation: a story of what such a trip would cost, for anyone who'd dare to follow me. Without breaking stride while we walked, I rattled off prices of everything from bottled water to gourmet pork chop sandwiches. Nicky skipped alongside, looking for a gateway into this game that his dad felt compelled to play. By the end of our trip, I intended for my reports to show which ballpark is the best bargain. This side project added a vague but reassuring sense of structure to the fourteen nights ahead of me.

I began to fill the tape with data my dad would admire, prices of food and drink as we walked past each stand, circling more than a mile around the concourse. "The Home Run Bakery. Carrot cake, cheesecake, $3. A brownie, a Snickers ice cream bar, $2."

Nicky played along, his voice on the tape chipping in costs of peanuts and cotton candy, and the Twizzlers sold in packages bigger than a folded sports section. Quickly, though, he became distracted by the scoreboard video race between red, yellow, and green colored dots. Graphics in 1994 were not much more sophisticated than Pac-Man. The dots roared through a course, trying to outflank each other before they crossed a finish line.

"Out of all the cheesy dot races everywhere, Ranger Stadium has the best," he said in a tone thick with sarcasm. "And green always wins."

There was losing ahead for us. Our trip's 81 scheduled innings began with a long inning for the Rangers. The long inning is a stretch of boundless game time where the team at bat hammers on opposing pitchers. In a long inning, batter after batter slams balls into the outfield for hits, or sprays them between lunging infielders. The team can draw walks and advance on wild pitches. Every team continues to hit until their team records a third out. Without a clock, baseball has no boundary for the battering a team must take. No three-run mercy rule.

We watched the reigning world champion Toronto Blue Jays pelt the Rangers for four runs in the top of the first. Texas was losing before some fans even found their seats. Despite the long strides of rookie Rusty Greer in right field or slugger Juan Gonzalez in left, the team couldn't catch easy chances to make outs. The Rangers' Billy Ripken, less-famous brother of Cal, bobbled a ball at second and another run crossed the plate. Three batters later, the shortstop muffed a grounder, and Texas was already down 4-0.

I was a sportswriter who'd turned to tech writing by that night, but I took notes throughout my vacation. I jotted them across the box score section and the margins of the sweat-stained blue lines of our Bibb Falk scorebook. I recorded each play on a page of the same Bibb Falk that held the record of Nicky's Little League season. Our Bibb Falk was to scorebooks as Webster's was to dictionaries. An Austin sporting goods store sold it. The 11x9 scorebooks, whose empty boxes run across rather than down, are as common to coaches and sportswriters as a No. 2 pencil is to the rest of the world. Ours wore a soft blue cover that evoked my college exam comp books. I'd been using a Bibb Falk since I first wrote sports for that suburban newspaper the year Nicky was born.

Paper was still the most portable recorder of details in 1994. Laptop was a new word applied to what most of us still called portable computers. Even as a tech reporter, I didn't own one yet. From some of our better seats during the trip I'd spy laptops open in the press boxes, the tools of seasoned sportswriters. Fancy, but with flaws. Those computers were at the mercy of the elements, the whims of batteries, and the errors of software. When a rainy inning would descend on us, nothing but a Bibb Falk would do. Damp paper still can carry memories. Although there's nothing easy about the access a Bibb Falk gives to storytelling—boxes on the page are half as big as a stamp to make notes on each batter—the scorebook is built to capture specifics.

Our Bibb Falk went onto the road with some pages already dog-eared, even though it was still in its first season. Springtime is the opening day for many scorebooks. Ours already bore marks of wet drink rings and the badges of mustard and ball field grime. Its metal spiral comb across the top was in fine working order, though.

I carried this notepad under my arm every time we passed through turnstiles to our seats. It was as essential as tickets. Paper outlined the path on our trip. With enough paper I wouldn't get lost on the road. And if time blurred memories, paper would help me find my way back. From small notes in the boxes of the Bibb Falk would come epic stories.

The pounding the Rangers were taking wasn't epic, but it was profound. Nearly a half-hour later, the Blue Jays' wrecking was done and noted on the pages of the book. Nicky smirked at me, cocking an eyebrow.

"What are you gonna do?" I said to him. "These Rangers are having a hard time keeping the Jays off the bases."

"Yeah, they're not playing too good right now," he said, with the glint of hope that comes from youth.

"Nice cup holders," I pointed out, trying to be a tour guide. I filled in some of the open squares that denote scored runs on my pad and tipped back my hat. "It'd help if they'd catch the balls hit right at them."

"It's only the first inning," he replied. "They can do better."

"Well, maybe," I said, trying to mirror his hope.

He slouched and pressed his feet into the seat back in front of him. It was only one game, but while I was bolting up the highway 200 miles to arrive in time for the National Anthem, I didn't leave room for the prospect of my team getting cuffed around. They were well behind on that hand-operated outfield scoreboard, another tribute to the ballparks of old. Camden Yards was the first tribute, but The Ballpark in Arlington was right behind it.

By the fourth inning the lure of the ballpark shops—there was one around every turn of the concourse—became too strong for my young consumer. We loped toward center field to the largest shop but also stopped at every souvenir stand along the way. In the main store, we wandered the aisles still full of mementos from the park's opening series. I'd been to ballparks from Boston to Baltimore and beyond, so I compared the costs of souvenir bats, those miniatures the size of nightsticks painted in team colors.

"The same size bat is $4 in Baltimore," I reported. "This is an inaugural year bat, though, so that's makes it $8 here in Texas."

"It's something like five bucks for the regular one," Nicky noted. "But the five-dollar one's ugly." The eight-buck bat went into our basket. A basket for a ballpark shop. Really.

On the recorder we counted up the bad values and good after our recitations of the dimensions of the ball field. The measurement, the comparisons, it helped me define where I was and how much fun might be had. It was my father's way, the analysis. The counting was fun, sure, but it was also my nervous tic, a habit of the heart.

Even during a game that cost some families more than $100 to attend, the shop was crowded. One small alcove gave the boys crowding around Nicky a place to marvel over the broken, chipped and certified bats of major leaguers. Eventually we picked up our first durable souvy, as we called them: a $13 "125th Year" Major League Baseball cap. MLB had swagger in 1994, even in the face of strike threats. I also bought a set of Ballpark in Arlington commemorative pins, marked down over the months since the glee cooled about the new park.

"Here's that great bat," Nicky said, approaching the register along with two t-shirts and a souvenir shot glass.

"Great," I said. "What else?" I was not going to be the dad who said no. I was manic enough in that moment to green-light nearly anything. Limits were for dads who weren't on epic road trips.

"There's this Canseco poster, too," he offered.

I felt the drive to be the dad of reason. "We'll never get that back in one piece after two weeks." I looked for a consolation prize. "How about trading card decks?"

Nicky came away from the counter with a couple of decks of ballplayers he could add to his fat collection back in Austin. They'd be at my house, I noted. After we finished shopping, we were standing near the outfield wall when a Ranger crushed a ball toward the centerfield fence. The sound of the crowd seemed to carry that ball toward us.

"Here it comes," Nicky called out as the crowd stood up in their bleacher seats in front of us "Dad, hold this."

I snatched his bag as he darted to the back of the centerfield rail. I lumbered after him. The blazing lights picked up the flight of the ball falling into the seats to our left. It bounced off the seats and fireworks rocketed off the top of the scoreboard behind us. The anthem from The Natural poured into the air.

"Yeah!" Nicky roared into the hot Texas night. He turned at me and pointed. "That's your boys! Hitting one. Going yard!"

The Rangers lost 7-5. The sweaty July crowd filed out, sedated like losers. When the game ended well beyond 10, we took pictures along the top level of the park. Only weeks later would I see how tired I looked.

We tooled over to the two-story Hilton across the highway, ready to rest for the hundreds of miles of driving the next day. I flexed my hands, gripping the wheel across the last few miles of driving from parking lot to hotel. Would our room still be available? I fretted. I'd done late check-ins before, but never solo on the road with my boy.

The game was a loss peppered with moments of glory and discovery. Tucked into the visor were those paper dot race tickets passed out by the ushers. On the back of each ticket was a coupon promising a free small soda at any local Whataburger. Hey, we could redeem it on the next day's drive as we left Texas.

FATIGUE SWEPT OVER ME AFTER THAT SWEATY REALITY. With my hand beside my pillow I drifted into sleep with a dreamy vision of my father's hands, the instruments he used to distribute anger and create magic. He'd run those hands over the top of a square valise, the one with tarnished metal corners and a leather handle stained from years of carrying. That case held his magic props. Like kids of my era I felt the sting from Dad's hands when I was bad, the spankings we dreaded worse than any pain they produced.

Dad's hands redeemed themselves at other times. He crafted magic more modern than the tricks in that valise. He built an electronics box he called the Blipper, a sound effects toy that my brother and I used as a soundtrack for our adventures with GI Joes and squads of green plastic Army Men. Dad's hands soldered the transistors, diodes, cast-off spare capacitors and other mystical components he'd pluck out of matchbook-sized plastic drawers on his workbench.

As I drifted into the twilight before sleep I wondered if Dad ever created what he wanted for himself. I had a dreamy vision of him at that workbench, staring at a project, not looking at me while I asked questions. Somehow I was back in that basement with him, trying to draw closer to the great and powerful R.E. Seybold.

He pressed his soldering gun onto those components on the bench. The smoke of the solder resin rose overhead to the planks and rafters beneath the living room floor. The click of that soldering gun in his hand switched on and then off.

"So what did you want, Dad?"

"Same as I want now. To be loved. Loved by somebody."

He never said anything like that when he was alive. I kept up the questions. "Loved by who?"

"The usual, dammit. My old man. My mother, before she died on me."

"She didn't love you?"

He pawed through a coffee can of resistors, holding each one up to scan its color-coded bands. The colors identified each resistor's power, and he read them as easily as a label on a box of Wheaties. He didn't answer me about his mom's love, but his silence did.

"But what about our mom? She loves you. I mean, she loved you." I was getting confused about talking to a man who was dead, but live as a bare electric wire in this exchange of truth.

"She said she loved me. Then she'd bitch and argue, not do what I said."

I turned away from Dad and toward the birch bookcase that I'd watched him stain by hand, a case with a folding glass door I loved to pull open. I tugged out a book called Popular Woodworking and closed the door quietly the way he liked.

"Whatcha got there, Ronny?" It was his old interrogating voice, but it sounded foggy, like shuffling a damp deck of cards.

"Popular Woodworking." It was the user manual and textbook for his multi-tool powerhouse of woodworking craft. "Mom sold the Shopsmith, you know."

"I figured she would. Good tool. Too bad."

I paged through the book slowly. "At least she waited until we were all gone, out of the house."

"Until I was gone, you mean."

I flipped the book open to its inside front cover. It was his, to be certain, because there was his rubber-stamped signature. "So how about us, Dad? I know I loved you. Even when you scared me, I just wanted it to stop, because I loved you."

He turned toward me, the change jingling in his pockets of his trousers he'd hike above his stomach. He pointed the soldering gun up away from his face, the same way he'd taught me to point his .22 rifle safely.

"Dad, you heard me, right? I said—"

"Yeah, that you loved me." He put the gun onto a bench that was spattered with solder. I thought he was going to hug me when he stepped closer. Then he rummaged in his trousers and pulled out his keys. His key-holder fob was a simple strip of chocolate-colored leather. It had a key ring sewed into one end, plus a snap that bound the fob to a ring on the other. He removed his keys and handed me the fob.

"If I'm so beloved to you, take this. It was mine. Now it's yours."

IN THE MORNING AT THE HILTON, HIS FOB rested on my nightstand. It became mine after he died. It was snapped to the keys of the Sunbird, with my Austin house key clipped on the other ring. I rolled over and reached for the Bibb Falk to tote up the game action from last night's loss. Whatever happened across the dozens of innings before us, I'd record it on the pages of our scorebook. No matter what else occurred, I believed I could trust the numbers.

My Bibb Falk could report that in a player's final at bat he slugged out a triple, a hit that sealed the win with a clutch RBI. Tiny flyspecks of notations, as personal as any stenographer's hand, fill a pad. Each scorekeeper has a voice on the pages that's theirs alone. The nuance paints details that sometimes only the writer can translate. I taught my scorekeeper dialect to Nicky on that trip. The danger in keeping so many notes, however, is that you'll miss witnessing a play as it happens while taking notes on the last.

Box scores—those summaries of each player's game results—are assembled on the right-hand edge of a Bibb Falk. I totaled up my first day. Plate appearances, runs, hits, RBIs, errors, strikeouts. The torrid trip departure with our top down, that was an out. My moves in the car weaving in the Arlington traffic, just a walk, but a safe appearance. Our spending in the gift shop—well, grounding into a double play. Then the disappointing game outcome and my grace about it, a clean hit. I scored a run when Nicky watched my team lose and saw me accept the loss. There were the easy runs, too, like that towering homer right at our feet, and the heart-thumping approach to the gates of a brand-new park for the first time in my life, the snap of those dogs in our seats along the first base line. With my team's loss, the trip was already imperfect. On Day One I went one-for-four with those runs and no errors. Acceptable. I wanted to do better the next day.

LOST ON A GETAWAY
Tigers vs. Royals
Kauffman Stadium, Kansas City
Saturday, July 16

Dad taught me that when done properly, vacation driving starts at dawn. I paced at sunup outside our Arlington hotel room, prowling the balcony and mulling over the day's driving. It felt daunting. The notes of the Star-Spangled Banner would float across our next ballpark in Kansas City at 7 that night. I was already anxious about whether Nicky and I would see the first pitch. First Pitch is the only moment in any ballgame ruled by a clock.

I tried to calm myself and shift my anxiety to excitement as the sun crept above the Arlington horizon. Daylight's burning, my dad would say. Our ballgame was more than eleven hours away. My trusty Triptik pages that I read on the balcony said Arlington was 561 miles away from Kauffman. I did the math and looked at my watch. I faced the first flaw of my manic plan: A need to leave early on the longest day of driving. Of course we could see two games in two nights in parks almost 10 hours' drive apart. No distance was too far. How else was this going to be the greatest trip ever? I could do this.

It was my first moment of feeling no backup. This trip had just one driver, a man who was already wide-awake with his passenger sleeping soundly on a morning of summer vacation. We came in so late from last night's game that nobody even brushed their teeth.

Our road on those two weeks would be ruled by the elements: earth and fire, air and water, and love. The earth lay everywhere in front of us, miles of asphalt that pointed to the Oklahoma horizon and beyond. Our car's cloth roof would shuck off the sun's fire. The air was all around me, cool AC billowing across our seats. We'd water our days with the roadside stops

I'd mete out like drinks from a dwindling canteen. But my primary element, essential to my anxious sacrifices, was love. It was as fundamental as carbon and as precious as gold.

I had our duffels packed by the time the sun came up. They would barely fit into the Sunbird's afterthought of a trunk. The Sunbird was fast enough to move like the wind, and on our first full day together I would need that speed. We had a chance to arrive by First Pitch, but only if we were on the move by 9. To push away the anxiety I had a plan. One gas stop of 15 minutes in Ardmore. Another in Emporia that could be no longer than that. Lunch at a McDonald's drive thru.

But I hadn't factored Saturday cartoons into my plan. What boy of eleven would want to walk out on Teenage Mutant Ninja Turtles, Sonic the Hedgehog, or Bugs Bunny? We'd created a habit of watching them together all morning on visitation weekends. To get to Game 2 I'd have to roust Nicky to cut off those cartoons and get him to dress. Not even a promise of a ballgame could speed his pace. I kept looking at my watch in its wide leather cuff on my wrist and muttered some words of parenting.

"C'mon, Nick. It's really time to go."

"Aw, just one more show."

"We're not going to make it in time."

"It's not that far away, and I haven't finished my breakfast yet." The hotel danish was scattered on his lap. He sat cross-legged on the rumpled polyester bedspread of the Hilton's decor, surrounded by beige walls and the stark daylight where the sun was already above the horizon.

"We'll have time for cartoons tomorrow."

"On Sunday? You're kidding, right?" He reached for the remote to switch the channel during a commercial.

I didn't want to yell, but the morning was slipping out of my grasp. I had to parent him, something that involved telling a son to do something he didn't want to do. "Okay, let's go." I took the remote off the bed where he set it and switched off the TV.

"Just one more cartoon, okay? Michelangelo's gonna pull 'em out of trouble." He took back the remote. "Then we can go."

"Okay, I guess we can wait a bit." This trip was supposed to be fun, after all.

I hauled our bags down the stairs and jammed them into the trunk. When I came back up Nicky was laughing. The danish was in his hand and he was nibbling on it absentmindedly. I paced and tapped my foot, standing in the doorway, looking over his shoulder. He turned to smile at me. I crept in to sit on the edge of the bed.

"Last one?"

"Okay." He snatched up the remote and switched off the TV when the commercial for Sugar Crisp started. When he moved toward the door he asked where his bag was.

"Already in the car."

"We're not late, are we?"

"No," I said. "But I have to drive a long way, and fast."

"Fast sounds great."

"And Michelangelo?"

"He saved the other Turtles, as usual." I stood at the door, ready to close it. "Wait. I gotta brush my teeth, right?" He must've seen me roll my eyes, while I was thinking about his toothbrush. Mine was already down in the car. "It won't take long. I put my toothbrush in the cup in the bathroom."

"And you have your own toothpaste?"

"You packed some. Right, Dad?"

More than a half-hour later we rolled onto Interstate 35. I was already doing the math, trying to figure out how to drive nine hours' worth of miles in eight.

I barreled past Plano and northward to Frisco, flirting with 75 as I slapped the Sunbird into fifth gear. Nicky was staring intently at his Game Boy, his eyes transfixed like they were on a morning five years earlier, another one when I had to pull his focus away from cartoons for an early departure. On that morning it was only me who was leaving, moving out of the home we shared as father and son. I was driving to my rented house as a divorced dad, a journey I'd been dreading for days.

I'd packed my bags and boxes the night before, moving them into my car after Nicky went to bed so he couldn't see my shamed face. I lingered on the carpet and listened to the sounds of Saturday morning. I shuffled slowly between our little brick house and my overstuffed Chevy Citation. The used cardboard cartons were stacked halfway up its windows, a car we got as a gift from my wife's father when her Toyota died. Now I'd take my first journey as a separated parent. I glanced out the aluminum storm door at those cartons, packed to overflowing with what I'd negotiated as mine. I craved tokens of my status as a dad. The divorce court would name me the Possessory Parent, the one whose rights expire at the end of the night of visitation. I was losing my everyday connection with my most precious possession.

I didn't understand any better than Nicky did why I couldn't live as an everyday dad. The sun shone bright on that December morning I had to leave him, casting long shadows over my heart. My father had failed to love out loud, as tight with his praise as with his dollars. I stood in that Austin doorway, unable to leave because I didn't know how to love out loud at times, at least not easily. I don't remember if Nicky knew how to ask where I was going or when I would come back. He was just shy of six.

With my free hand I picked up a lump of Play Doh from the beige carpet.

"Daddy, can you stay for cartoons?"

His voice had a familiar ring, the one he used when I was leaving for work during the week. But on this Saturday, dressed in his Ninja Turtle pajamas, he sat cross-legged in front of our massive 27-inch TV.

"I want to, Nicky," I started. He turned to gaze at me with those great brown eyes, set in a face that mimicked my own baby pictures. This was part of the ritual we played out during his first six years. "Can you stay?" really meant, "Do you love me?" and my reply assured, "You know I do."

He had changed my life. Before I was a dad I thought I could see all of my life before me, but that shifted the day he was born. When the doctor turned that tiny head toward me during the delivery, I saw the boy inside myself, a face that mirrored mine. I knew on that day my future could have a brighter expression. I believed on the day of his birth I could provide a strong set of shoulders to lift that little head high. He'd see further than I did. A half-dozen years into his new life, my Rockwell painting was streaked with tears.

"Will I see you tonight?" he asked, not looking away from *Transformers*. The bowl of Captain Crunch was not far from his knee. I paused too long to answer, and he turned away from cartoons to look at me.

"Daddy, will I?" I thought the voice had a tremble in it, one I heard as an echoing rumble in my heart.

"Not tonight, Nicky. Daddy's not going to come home tonight."

"Then when will I see you?"

I knew the answer just by looking out the storm door at everything I'd jammed into the car. "In a few days, buddy. Your mom will stay here with you."

"Where will you be?"

"I'm going to live in another house, Nicky. You can come and visit me there."

He turned back to the cartoons. "Mighty Mouse is on next," he announced in an eager voice. "We always watch Mighty Mouse, Daddy. Sit down," he added, and tugged at my blue jean leg. I set down my keys and crouched in place with him next to the crusting-over bowl of Captain Crunch's remnants.

Nicky had heard the fighting during the previous months, the shouted pain that bounced off the dark brick fireplace at the other end of the room. My marriage to his mom wasn't going to survive that anger. But there was a deeper wound from the cut than losing my lover and mate. I was learning how deep losing anybody could cut.

"Nicky, I'm not going to be living with you anymore," I said, blurting the words past the ache in my chest.

"This is about stupid-o divorce," he said in a little while, then reached out with a sticky hand to touch my beard. It was a gentle act, one he liked to do while I gave him his bath. Tonight that bathtime ritual would happen without me in his house. I thought of those tiny fingers in his very first bath, just minutes old in the hospital. I had washed him with the gentlest touch I could manage then, marveling at the miniature masterpiece I'd made with his mother. I beamed when I heard the nurse's praise on that day.

That was a memory I didn't need to recall in the moment of my departure. His mother and I agreed we weren't matched for each other, and a better life lay on separate paths. But my path would have fewer of Nicky's Ked-prints on it, each one scheduled from today onward, meted out by a court decree whose rules were called standard and customary all over the legal papers.

"Yes, it's about divorce, Babbo. But I still love you very much."

"So why can't you stay?"

I picked up his Play Doh. "We have to live in separate places from now on. I'll still see you on some weekends, and…"

"I hate this," he started, and then he looked at the tears in my eyes. "Don't cry, Daddy. I still love you, Babbo." He hung his own pet name back on me, the name I sang to him in the quiet lullaby I devised when I'd walk him back to sleep as an infant, dangling over my shoulder. In the smallest of the night hours when he struggled to sleep in his own bed, I sang him to safety with that song. He was a Ninja Turtle by day, but always Babbo by night.

I kissed his forehead and picked him up as I stood. The pain in my chest had nothing to do with Nicky's weight. I held him tight. "Let's watch Mighty Mouse together," I told him through a too-bright smile. "I don't have to go just yet."

He took the Play Doh from my sweaty palm, reshaping it with insistent strokes of kneading in his small hands.

HALFWAY ACROSS OKLAHOMA, AFTER A BIG MAC and a Quarter Pounder, Slim Jims from that Diamond Shamrock station in Ardmore, and Big Gulps crowding our cup holders, the plan became obvious. I should have scheduled a travel day. First Pitch was going to be out of our reach. I was sure of it. I was a complete reader of every game's story. I was dedicated enough to read the foreword, introduction and appendix of each game: batting practice, the game action and fleshing out scorecards with stats through all nine innings complete, until the security guards came to kick us out of our seats. Even if we had to miss the foreword of batting practice, a real fan always made it to the park by First Pitch. I glanced at my watch. First Pitch, ruled by a clock.

Be honest, I told myself while I drove, it's not so crazy what you're trying to do today. You didn't really want to throw away one of only two Saturday nights of this trip to some stop in mid-Kansas on some travel day. So we drove like militia fugitives across an endless march of low grass, mustard-brown plains, and the arrow-straight Interstate roads that shot through the reservations of Oklahoma. We stopped, but like men pursued by a posse. Less than 90 minutes of that drive was memorable. I swept the convertible through the swales of the Flint Hills outside Wichita. As we lost the sunlight amid those hills, I switched on the Sunbird's brights to find our way to home plate. Nicky nodded off and I could listen to my own music, Sinatra's hits. It was my father's favorite music, and for a little while he was there with me, listening to Frank serenade us through the swells of the ranch land. A falling sun paraded dramatic shadows along those rounded hilltops pressed from nature's bustier. As daylight disappeared, the car was galloping at 80 on Interstate 70.

I was echoing my boyhood experience with this frantic pace. Arriving anywhere late—or just at a time Dad did not anticipate—was cause for calamity. My dad considered his driving schedule as inviolate as the 11th Commandment, Thou Shalt Not Go Off Schedule. In our Sunbird, unlike that family white station wagon, nobody was going to yell about it if we didn't make it there in time. I was resolute about being relaxed.

In my muddled mapping, I'd counted the miles to the Kansas City in Kansas, a handful of exits short of the Missouri edition of KC. Then Kauffman was a half-dozen exits beyond that city as well. The atlas was less than perfect. I squirmed after we pulled into the endless parking lot. Then I'd parked in the Chiefs' Arrowhead football stadium, one we would have to cross before entering Kauffman's lot. I could hear the lineups of the Tigers and the Royals being announced as we peeled ourselves out of sweaty car seats.

First Pitch might still be in reach, though. We stretched our legs from the long drive by bounding through the parking lot at breakneck speed. I scampered for the restroom, juggling the scorebook, my butt-pack, and keys. I needed something more desperately than the sound of the National Anthem. I needed to stand up in a restroom for a while before I could sit down.

"Dad, aren't we going to find our seats?"

"Yeah, sure. But first I gotta make a pit stop."

"Oh, okay. Can I go down there then?"

"Hey, come with me." I waited at the door of the restroom.

"I just wanna go to my seat." I'd have to meet him there. It would be the first time we'd sit down at a ballpark separately. He was growing up and this was another rite of my passage. He wouldn't get lost or stolen. He was sharp enough to avoid the former. I mustered the faith he'd be lucky enough to escape the latter.

One thing hasn't changed across the history of baseball. Hours of empty time parade across any game night. Most three-hour games have less than 20 minutes of action. Even while we sat in the lower bowl enjoying the play, there was ample time to think about someone else, or talk about something completely outside of the game. We parked ourselves in the shiny green plastic seats. I waited for my ass to stop vibrating from the driving. The colored lights over the famous center field water feature lulled me. I didn't pick Kaufmann because of its well-known fountains, which in 1994 were the only ones in the majors. We weren't close enough to hear the waters, even though there was less chatter in the crowd than in Arlington.

A banner hung along the third base line touting a nationwide TV show, *Baseball Across America*. In the years before "live look-ins," one broadcast network had a similar idea. NBC's viewers got a taste of selected games on a Saturday night, then the network moved on to another ballpark. Growing up with a dad who worked at an NBC station, I took it as an article of faith that TV coverage made anything more important.

"We might be seen on nationwide TV," I said to Nicky.

He was catching us up, filling in the boxes for the team lineups. "Yeah?" He said it without looking up.

"Well, television's one way things become more real."

"What do you mean? We're really here."

"Yeah, but we can be with a lot of other people at the same time. Because of the TV." I saw him look up and search my face for what I meant. "I don't know. Maybe it's just that way for people..." I was about to say "my age," but I wasn't ready to become my dad, carping about the differences between younger people and my generation. I needed to be Nicky's buddy in that moment.

We had supper in our seats, stuffing ourselves with a Kansas City concoction: a mound of tater tots smothered with local delicacy Gates Barbecue. It was too sinful and delicious to leave a morsel uneaten, even though there had already been Carnation malted milkshakes (frozen hard in paper cartons) as appetizers. The Kansas City beef must have been slow cooked, since it didn't require more than a gentle push of a flimsy plastic fork to separate it into bites.

A word here about food, an indulgence every night that made its way to a sin. Some cities were known for specialties we'd never heard of. Cincinnati would have Cincinnati chili, made with spaghetti noodles under a ground beef chili. Food like that was an unexpected gift, because in 1994 there was no easy research to set up anticipation. On some game nights I'd go forage while Nicky scored. I'd return with something like onion rings that were both crisp and spicy. I didn't have to leave the game action, though. In every ballpark there were vendors plying the aisles. I learned the trust of paying with a crisp $20 bill, passed from one fan to the next and to the vendor, then watching the change passed back. It opened my world and Nicky's too. You could trust strangers to handle your money if a dog or a beer or a funnel cake was a part of the exchange.

Twenty runs later, the Royals had suffered a 13-7 loss. We had a reserved hotel room downtown—another late check-in—but finding it in the dark was another matter. I had only my Triptik and Rand McNally atlas in the car, bolstered by a folded map with only major city streets. We drove in a world without GPS.

The sound of the crowd in the lot turned rougher while my dashboard clock ticked toward midnight. I turned on the overhead and squinted at the map's red and black lines. The atlas was of no help for the miles just beyond that parking lot. The right way wasn't on a map, but I skimmed details of the page. The Triptik and atlas were my safety railings. We needed to find that Best Western hotel, three stars in the AAA Guidebook, before the pounding in my chest took over.

After two streets I stopped at a light and turned toward the soothing whoosh of the Interstate. I followed an underpass below I-70 and then scanned the streets to the left and right. In any brand-new city, I have a knack for finding the Worst Part of Town. It's like radar that steers me into tough neighborhoods. It doesn't take more than a few turns, as it did that night, to find a place where I could smell the scent of danger.

I drove right past one exit ramp, seeing the beaming badge of the Interstate too late. I panicked as I saw grimy curbs and windshields of aging sedans. I pulled past an intersection with its traffic light going stale, green to yellow, and plowed forward. No place to look at a Triptik map. That was not the time to mince through the blocks that had shifted from bright streetlights to stretches where neon and tavern beer signs showed the way.

Nicky teased me about our bandanas being gang colors, and I tried to keep my composure. Suddenly, the glow of lights over a used car lot revealed a ramp. The Interstate badge shimmered like a shrine. We escaped onto the white bread lanes of I-70. I'd blown up any of my remaining aura of fatherly expertise.

My ghetto radar humbled me. My Little Leaguer giggled in a release full of happiness and teasing. Safe at our mainstream motel, I hung my damp jersey and shorts on a wall rack, a faux-closet behind the door. I could make a colossal mistake and nobody would yell. Relief washed over me. Life wasn't perfect. And it didn't have to be.

JOYSTICKS AND SIDEARMS
Travel Day
Sunday, July 17

I slept beyond first light for the first time in days. My background worries—steady companions that often jab me out of sleep—all settled into the shadows on that morning. I woke before Nicky, though, a habit throughout the trip. I pulled on wrinkled cargo shorts and an orange t-shirt with a mustard stain on the pocket, then slipped into leather sandals. No sneakers today. This would be a day without a First Pitch deadline, a travel day. I was supposed to be on a vacation, the most special ballpark trip ever. I would not be weary tonight. All I had to do was drive east and north and enjoy a summer day with my son.

It felt bracing to wake up and see beige. The sensation in my chest, that quicker heartbeat of an anxious man, lifted me into elation. The hotel was not plush, not on my budget. The Best Western Seville Plaza was just a motel clad in polyester comforters and dusky brown no-shag carpets. The colors delivered comfort beyond the fresh sheets, a contrast with the colors of those midnight streets we'd escaped. I congratulated myself on navigating what surely might have been a deadly moment. Such needless drama came all too easy in any unfamiliar setting. I'd avoided a meltdown during that ghetto blunder. Maybe I could be trusted to be in charge at my worst.

I slipped out the door so as not to wake my boy. Nicky wouldn't rise for much of any weekend noise except cartoons. My steps carried me toward the newspaper box downstairs. A story would be in the pages of the *Kansas City Star*. Hemingway's old paper, I told myself, should be a pretty good read.

The rising sun lit the close-parked cars in the motel's pebble-paved lot out in front. The paper box rested inside a short black metal fence. Protection and safety—yes. I bounded down the stairs two at a time. My anxiety forced me to check that I'd locked the Sunbird. The car stood exactly where I parked it, unviolated. I grabbed a paper and ran back to the room, in case Nicky did wake unexpectedly. We had five years of weekends already under our belt. Being out of his earshot when he woke up in a strange city might be too scary—for him and for me.

The change in my fanny pack jingled as I toted the ballgame story up to our room. I would read it to Nicky once he woke up. No hurry on this Sunday. After 972 miles along our journey, we'd earned our day of rest. I heard my rebel voice inside, the one that shucked off all of my Catholic guilt and duty. Remember, you're out playing now. Find a way to enjoy this slower day. Even pro ballplayers have travel days without a game. This Sunday night would be different in another, better way. Nicky wouldn't be leaving at the end of this weekend.

We often wore our colors as part of one of our game-day routines, replica jerseys of our teams. I had a Reds jersey, old Ohio boy that I am, and Nicky wore his Little League Cubs jersey. But after the heat of the last two afternoons, my jersey already smelled like a locker room. It would probably smell no better when I put it on in Cincinnati. In the mirror I saw the mustard on my worn-thin tee from Tony Packo's—a restaurant in my Toledo hometown, four days away. I was always aware of what was on my horizons.

Nicky hadn't been back to Toledo since he was six. His toddler Toledo cousins would be pre-teens by now. I could show off how much my son had grown since the family last saw him. It would be chest-puffing time, out on my own with him and parenting solo, a counterpoint to my divorce.

I folded the newspaper under my arm and got on the hotel elevator. The hum of the elevator reminded me of the sound of a VCR. On my last trip to Toledo I toted a video camera everywhere along with my son. Once we got back I was fast-forwarding the tape for Nicky's mom, cueing it up to a spot I was sure she'd enjoy. Nicky was giggling and playing with his cousins in the basement of my brother Bob's mid-city bungalow. It was close quarters in there under the stairs. The kids didn't care.

But my ex-wife did. I studied her face while she watched the movie, hoping to see her smile.

"What's wrong?" I asked.

"It's so small in there," she said. "Dark, too."

"They're having fun though."

She lit up one of her Virginia Slims. "I just realize we're so different, you and me."

"What do you mean?" I felt my chest getting tight, heard my voice rising.

"It's so old, and it's probably dirty under those steps."

"You weren't there. And it's a basement. You didn't grow up with basements. When I was growing up, we played in them. They're supposed to be a little dirty.'

"Not for my son."

"He's my son, too." I paused the video. "I took him back to my home, my brother and sister's places. He played with his cousins. You didn't have any of those, either."

"You really don't have to get angry, do you?"

I threw the video remote across the room. "You can't even understand what you see right in front of you, on that screen. They're laughing."

"Dirty and dark. That's where he goes when you watch him."

"We weren't brought up by maids, at least. We saw our mother all day, I mean, every day."

"And I can see how much good that did you." She stubbed out her cigarette and I felt sparks of fear. She really was going to leave me.

As the Best Western's elevator doors parted, the ding pulled me back into my Sunday. I walked down the beige hallway while I scanned the game story. I tossed it on Nicky's bed and saw he was already awake, somehow.

"Where's breakfast, Dad?" He wasn't annoyed, just genuinely curious.

"Downstairs, down the street, anyplace we want."

"Mc-D's?"

"Something else, this morning. Denny's?" My old hangout from after my nights on the stage. He said okay, that a ballpark vacation meant everything could be different.

I thumbed through the AAA guidebook. I skimmed it while I re-did my counting. Nine games over eleven days on the schedule. Even after the first two days' worth of miles, the next seven games were spread across a schedule as busy as any major leaguer's. Wake in one city, with a game waiting in another. We'd have just a single no-game day over the next week.

"Some game last night," he said when the quiet in the room got deep. "Tigers really ripped 'em up with that fourth inning. The whole place getting so quiet after Fryman's grand slam went out."

"Not to mention Gibson's."

"Three runs scored, two for three including that homer. Pretty good for an old guy."

The Tigers outfielder was my age. "The balls flew out, sure. So did your dad's sense of direction afterward."

"It's okay. More silly than scary. Wearing colors, wow." He looked at my paper folded back to the game story. "Okay, I know you want to read it out loud. Be the sportswriter you were, Dad. You know you love it." I announced the game story, trying to keep it below a volume too loud for a Sunday.

My dad didn't care about being too loud on any of our blistering, up-tempo family vacations. He believed getting to a destination according to plan was at least as crucial as any event after arrival. To avoid the delays of roadside stops, my brother and I would pee in a Folgers coffee can. The scent of the piss felt naughty before we capped the can off with the plastic lid. Dad had three kids to manage on those trips, instead of just one boy like I did. Of course, he used my mom as emotional backstop. Dad threw wild pitches of anger, maybe because he was weary from his worries. We had that in common. Being tired was dangerous.

No one would grow weary on this Sunday. Our easy pace meant we'd drive fewer than 300 miles and still get halfway to Cincinnati and Riverfront for our next game. We'd cut deeper into the Midwest and be in Illinois before sundown, ready for the Monday to follow. I was already calculating my route into the future when this Sunday had only just begun.

We searched for morning cartoons in vain. It was the lazy start that Nicky hoped for on Saturday when cartoons were plentiful. Even with low-grade cable in the hotel there was no Ninja Turtles, Scooby Doo, or the Animaniacs on this Sunday. We'd leave earlier than yesterday. We pulled our duffels down to the car. Since it was cloudy, the top came down. Our game caps went on and the scent of sunblock rose up off our necks. We'd play our day's only game at lunch.

We crested the Ozarks and crossed the Missouri River after Booneville. I managed to stop watching the dashboard clock. It was a travel day with no First Pitch to worry about. It started to feel like a real vacation with the top down and broken cloud cover keeping us cooler. Once we drove toward a town called Kingdom City it felt like lunchtime. We gassed up at a 7-11 there and I pulled burritos off the tray next to the checkout. Then Nicky found the video games at the back of the store.

"Hey Dad, NBA Jam! Let's play."

"Sure, here's a couple of quarters."

"Really? C'mon. You gotta play, too."

NBA Jam? I could barely keep up in Pac Man. This game had a whole other level of expertise. Trick moves, multiple touchpads. Nicky knew it cold from the evenings I took him to the Tilt arcade in the mall. I read the joy in his face on our Sunday like a hymnal. Baseball games did this at times, but playing a game is richer than watching one if you know the game.

He took Shaq and left me with Barkley. A couple of games later I was road kill. I started thinking about the road and walked back to the counter. I needed beer nuts and Doritos to keep myself entertained while driving.

At the console, Nicky's laughter mingled with the game's announcer. "He's heating up," the game roared, and then "He's on fire!" Nicky's laughs echoed the sound from under those stairs with his cousins years earlier. "Boomshakalaka!"

I walked back to see him spinning the console joystick, jabbing at the shot buttons. The noise battled with the sounds of the Cardinals game on KMOX behind the counter. I thought of Cincinnati's Riverfront and felt hungry to get there, hungry in a way no 7-11 burrito could satisfy.

"Dad, can I play a few more?"

My dad would say we were already falling behind. Then I thought of that breakneck pace of his. He wanted to show us the world, but those vacations could never contain all the stops he'd dream up. Was this one of those hurried days for Nicky and I? After I took one step away from the console I saw Nicky's face fall.

I sailed back to the counter. "Gimme some quarters for this," I said to the clerk, handing him a fiver. I took the fistful of coins and handed it over to Nicky.

"You can play these." He beamed. "But you'll get to keep anything that you don't play." I bounced my eyebrows and winked. I had a scheme to bribe him to walk away from the game, but my wink was lost on him as he raced back to the console. On the radio the Cardinals played all the way through the bottom of the second while I played NBA Jam with my boy. My Barkley finally did beat his Shaq in one game. Only one, and Nicky let me win. I'd take that win, however it arrived. It was unplanned fun, not mapped out months in advance. It also left Nicky in control for that hour of the trip—of his time and of a little money as well.

Those game sounds proved I was having a better time than my dad enjoyed with us on the road. Five dollars wasn't much in 1994. Our road spending followed the Way of the Interstate: you spent foolish money while you were on the move, running from the boredom of limited-access highways. My dad only had money enough to provide us one vacation a year. Every moment had to count.

Counting money made him doubt his ability to provide. By the time we were all born, he was years removed from being a teenager in his classic serviceman picture, dressed in his fresh Navy blues and smiling with hope for a war adventure. He first took on fatherhood as stepdad to my older half-brother John, then as the dad of a firstborn son who lived only three days. I arrived the year Dad turned 30. A little more than a year later he fathered my brother Bob. The scant fifteen months between us made us Irish twins. Three years later my sister was born, so before Dad was 35 he'd had three new kids in four years' time. It became fatherhood duty that was well above Dad's pay grade. He cared for us with his paycheck and his workshop and the tool chest in the garage. He craved control over a house with three small kids, stenciling his name on one side of that toolbox and "Hands Off" on the other.

Nicky rocked at the NBA Jam joystick with a wide grin on his face. I sifted through my memories to recall a few smiles from Dad, laughing at TV comics, or mugging for the Super 8 camera on those rare times he'd let Mom hold it. The memories flowed off the three-minute home movies from trips like the one to Montreal for Expo 67. With three kids aged 6 through 10, my parents packed us into a compact station wagon. That Valiant wagon had a blue interior, just like the Sunbird's.

Even when Dad wasn't lost, Mom would ask if he was sure we were headed in the right direction. He never stopped to ask for directions, although he could see Mom was worried. She didn't trust him, and maybe he didn't trust himself completely. He'd led us all astray one time in Rochester, following the same Worst Part of Town radar he must have passed on to me.

We buzzed along trying to find the New York Turnpike. "On these bad streets with all the coloreds, for God's sakes," Mom said.

"Dammit," he shot back, "you can't expect me to ask for directions and keep us on schedule."

"Bob, you can't make that left turn. It's one-way."

"I knew that," he said as he straightened the wheel with a jerk of his wrists. "Let's just get back to the turnpike and start over." Mom folded back the map in summer morning's light. "You're going to say we missed a turn now, aren't you?"

"Well, we should have turned left."

I sat in the back and watched. Could he threaten her with a swing while both hands were busy with the driving? I knew he'd never pull over to make a point. It'd spoil his schedule.

Mom slumped in her seat as we slowed, Dad eyeing the road signs and just glancing at the traffic lights. She turned to see us punching each other in the back seat, pinching and laughing to distract ourselves.

"You kids quiet down back there," Dad roared, "or I'll turn this car around."

"Dad, didn't you turn it around once already?" I asked it in the most innocent voice I could concoct. He was too busy to spot my sarcasm. Mom let out a laugh, though.

"Daddy," my sister asked, "are we lost?"

"Ask your mother. She knows everything." He motored us onto the highway, but then the road toward the turnpike sailed up on our right. "Damn it, there's the turn." He pumped the brakes and cut the wheel hard to the right while the exit sign came up fast.

"God almighty, watch it!" Mom grabbed the back of her bench seat as the wagon careened into the turn.

"Cool, Dad. You lifted those wheels right off the ground," I said. My brother uncorked a breathy laugh and peeled himself off of the door.

Dad chuckled. "Not bad, if I say so myself." I saw him grin at Mom, whose color was just returning to her face. "We're not lost now, are we?"

"Let's stop up here at the exit coming up," she said. "There's going to be somebody there to ask about directions."

"You just want to empty the coffee can," I blurted. "Right, Mom?"

"Be quiet back there," she said with a yell that revealed her fright. "We're lucky we're not all killed."

Put your eye out with a stick, crack your head wide open, get yourself killed: on our childhood roads, the danger and drama were no more than one hard turn away.

NICKY AND I ROLLED PAST MONTGOMERY CITY, then Wentzville and through the maze of four interstates that spanned St. Louis. The Cardinals were playing on the road, or otherwise we'd have been sitting in Busch Stadium. But that Cardinals game stayed strong on the Sunbird's radio for more than an hour until we drove out of range. Nicky started up the Stone Temple Pilots after the game faded. He dug into his paperback *Goosebumps* while I kept looking at our odometer, brushing back the cobwebs of fatigue.

I faced brushback pitches in the earliest days of my divorce, especially at the start of Nicky's first baseball season. I felt like his mom was working to keep me away from home plate. After we'd tossed love together at the start, she'd become the pitcher throwing tight inside, pushing me away from Nicky with the close pitches baseball calls chin music. She didn't trust me, didn't even like me. She had good reasons. I let my work as a provider distract me, hustling for my boy. I told myself Dad's lie, that providing was enough.

In baseball, whenever you argue about balls and strikes it never goes any better for the rest of the game. You can get tossed. At the brink of Nicky's first Little League season, his mom was slow to sign a release to permit him to play. It was only coach-pitch ball, plenty safe. Nobody was going to get beaned. I could not be certain, but one thing that may have felt unsafe to her was expecting to see me at all of his games. I certainly planned to be at every one. Those games were the extra innings with my son. I was a rookie dad who'd started to mature, eager for more at-bats. In Nicky's first season I had to run right through signs like a runner ignoring a third base coach: her hard looks at me whenever I'd stop after a game to get a hug from him as he left the field.

While she relented she added conditions to his play. If a game didn't fall on a visitation night or one of my weekends, she didn't want me talking to him. I sometimes respected her wishes, but she couldn't keep me from shouting encouragement from the stands. Like a dug-in batter, I'd foul off her tight pitches to stay alive. She could strike me out, because whenever there was any event she wanted him to attend, he'd miss a game. She was pitcher and umpire all at once. I tried to make my clean hits of connection with him.

As the darkness fell over the Illinois countryside, I measured my forgiveness for her too-wide strike zone. I'd chipped away at her big lead in authority. Baseball has improbable comebacks, because a team never runs out of time at the end. It's all about the outs remaining. I got my comeback because Nicky's stepdad loved baseball like I did. Baseball was a way for both of us to connect with Nicky.

That first season was safe enough for a second one, a step up because this time the kids pitched the games. I could make some father and son talk out of that season which had just ended. I wanted to relive those games.

"You didn't get hurt at all this year, did you?" In the growing dark, I could still see Nicky put down his Game Boy.

"Hurt? No."

"Not even when you caught in that game?"

"I had shin guards, a helmet, and a mask."

"Yeah. I'll never forget the way you flipped back that helmet and mask to get an eye on that one pop up. Like you'd done it all your life."

"Just saw it on TV, you know."

I scanned the road signs, looking for a marker toward a motel. We had no reservations. "And then there was your saved game. 'For the championship,' like we always used to say on Cut Grass Field." Cut Grass was my nickname for the little patch of front yard where we played on visitation weekends. I held onto the name after Nicky was too big to play ball in that yard. We used the Chinese talla trees as bases.

There were moments of his baseball failure I overlooked. Nicky fell apart when he hurled his first pitches off the tawny soil of the Northwest Little League mound. As a starter he got rocked by hits and a homer, plus he walked batters. In the season's finale he returned as a relief pitcher, closing down the hitters in the growing twilight of a winner-take-all game. I wanted to praise his mastery of that night, the good fortune so unexpected.

"I loved the way you pitched that night. Sidearm, baby." I could talk about his style of curveball in the dark of the car and he wouldn't see me well up with prideful tears. "That closer, he breathes baseball like a marlin takes in seawater," I intoned, mimicking the Tigers announcer Ernie Harwell. "His hair curls out in mustard-colored locks from under the Cubs cap."

"I guess I was good that night," he said, reaching for a packet of sunflower seeds. Nobody in the car cared about the mess. "Not sure why I was good."

"You were redeeming yourself." It was quiet in his seat, often his response to my praises. "I mean, getting yourself even after that blow-up the time you started. It was beautiful."

I was winding up to pitch I'm-proud-of you's, the words I wanted so badly from my dad. I shifted to my Harwell voice, smooth as the drawl we heard that afternoon from the voice of the Cardinals, Jack Buck. "He looks calm, blowing bubbles with his Big Chew gum between pitches. He slings his arm low along the ground as he throws. They're sidearm strikes, tough to see until it's too late, even at the moment they cross the plate."

During that magic inning while Nicky pitched, the batters seized up to watch third strikes flash by, or whiffed and missed. I paced the bleachers and then came down to the backstop fence for a snapshot. The picture on my wall in my home office shows Nicky in mid-stride on the mound. He's capturing heroics after a start in failure, pitching better at a game's ending than at the beginning.

"Hey, here's something," I said when a road sign arose in the Illinois dark. "Maybe here in, what is it? Vandalia."

"Yeah, but don't miss the exit." There was a giggle. "We're wearing colors." We found an unplanned Days Inn off Exit 6e in an inky night. Maybe this beige hotel on the open prairie was a sign.

Pitchers throw to win, but sometimes a starter only pitches well enough to prevent the worst. They leave when a game isn't decided, so the outing is called a no-decision. As we settled in at the Days Inn, I felt like I was earning a win as a reliever after my rocky innings as a starting parent.

In our room, I called Dottie while I watched TV alongside Nicky. Avoiding the motel's pricey long distance, I pawed my way through sixteen digits of a dial-in access code on the clunky nightstand phone. She was in Seattle for her sister's wedding, and the usual night-before marriage drama was landing in my wife's lap. She couldn't talk, so I hung up crestfallen.

The motel TV had Cinemax, and in my sulking I forgot to change the channel as it switched over to late night shows. Nicky got a dose of what we learned to call Skin-e-Max. He just took in the skin like an 11-year-old boy would, maybe knowing it was taboo. I told myself after I switched it off that he wouldn't report my bad judgment to his mom. That night I wasn't much better at parenting than a teenaged babysitter. I'd try to make up for my error in our next game day.

CONCRETE BALKS
Marlins vs. Reds
Riverfront Stadium, Cincinnati
Monday, July 18

Monday morning was a happier starting point for this Custody Dad when I was riding the roads with my son. The day's drive would be a swing through some of Indiana, a bit of Kentucky, and then on into Cincinnati. Riverfront Stadium lay just across an Ohio River bridge, a few miles into the state where I was born.

I watched Nicky smile as we got closer to Riverfront and could see an echo of his shining cherub cheeks from a backyard picture. On a summer day eleven years earlier, my infant son sat in the grass of the Ohio backyard where I'd first learned to catch a baseball. My gauzy vision of family wasn't tarnished yet on that day in that yard. Before the gates could open on the Reds ballpark, I was determined I would be that happy again while in Ohio.

We pulled off Pete Rose Way into the parking lot in the late afternoon. The sun was brilliant and the air crisp after an overnight rainstorm. This was not really a ballpark; it was a stadium built for both football and baseball. There was no expanse of grass, just AstroTurf carpeting. It was a monolith of concrete, modernistic but soulless from the outside as well as in the seats. Six dollars gave me the pick of any spot for the Sunbird in a field of asphalt that held only a smattering of cars. We snatched our gloves and the Bibb Falk and quick-timed it up to the gates.

"Aw, not open until 5:30," Nicky said. "What'll we do?" He stood at the entrance with the glove under his arm. The glove was for any foul balls that might drift over our seats.

"Just wait, I guess."

"Hey, how about we throw?"

"In the parking lot?"

"Sure," he said. "We can do that, right?"

"Sure." Playing catch with him wasn't on my schedule for that day, but I was happy to oblige. Nicky and I practiced our baseball, a game of catch that glimmered with a happy memory from my dad. He and I played catch often enough until I was about Nicky's age. Dad never moved much when he threw, and I remember watching him lean to the left and right to catch. I wondered what Nicky might ever remember about my throwing form.

We returned to the Sunbird to fetch our ball and tossed across open parking spaces. First 20, then 30, then 35. Not every throw was on target, and when either of us missed we'd have to sprint after the ball. The asphalt took that bounce of the ball and launched it with a leap, bounding across the painted lines.

"Ho, and it gets away from Vizquel at short," I said, chasing after the scuffed ball.

"The runner is rounding third," Nicky said. "He's heading for home."

"And here comes the throw." I sailed the ball high and slow, instead of the bullet of a pitch that a shortstop would need after missing a catch. Nicky leapt up to grab my throw, then tossed it right back to me.

"For the double play," he shouted.

I stretched for the ball to my left to snag it. It felt good because we'd put in four hours of driving. I was stretching myself into improvisation there in the lot, making up fun in an unplanned place. A group of bros leaned against a brown Nissan pickup, watching us.

"Got him at second," I said. "What a bullet from Johnny Bench."

"Hey, you mean Alomar," referring to the Indians' All-Star catcher.

I walked the ball back to him. "Naw, the only catcher you mention in this town is Johnny Bench." When I was Nicky's age the Reds two-time champion, All-Star and Hall of Famer was my hero. Smart, passionate, and with a great arm. I imagined my son as all three.

"Some more," Nicky said. "They won't let us in yet."

"Sure," I said. "Let's do some flies." With the ball tossed high into the air, we started to catch more of them instead of chasing the misses. I watched the ball drop into his glove with a thud, thinking to myself that these fly balls were probably something he didn't have with his stepdad when they visited

Wrigley. I didn't want to know if I was wrong.

"Wait up," I said. "Let me get back to my place."

I trotted back to my spot in the lot, counting out the spaces. The scrape of my tennis shoes on the gray asphalt was a sound I never heard Dad make with a baseball in hand. On our sessions of catch he threw wearing his cordovan wing-tips. Dad only pulled on soft-soled shoes while on our 16-foot boat, or when he'd pushed the Toro across the lawns. He was a dad in the era when fathers mowed instead of exercised. He'd never bounded across any parking lots with me. Baseball was supposed to be played on grass.

AT BREAKFASTS ON THE MORNINGS BEFORE DAD would push that Toro, I'd sit beside him while he'd eat two eggs sunny side up. The yolks were shining with butter the way Dad liked and perched beside crisp strips of bacon. His diet didn't bring him down, though. It was his anger that hacked at his health and wounded my heart, too. During our worst evening we roared through a fight—combat that an overconfident boy like me, nearly 18, could spark from a dad who never was wrong about anything.

I already finished two college semesters that he'd paid for. I was simmering in his house for a year after high school, stewing under his resigned gaze while I took my opening jab at college. Choosing to work toward a degree was never questioned. The Seybold family included no university graduates. My ride into college would be on Dad's money. He didn't know how to express interest in my schooling without adding a layer of critique. I'd had enough of those opinions.

A year of college hadn't given me a career dream. I started in the local college studying to be an engineer like Dad, but a degreed one. Better than he did, I figured. He watched me land with thud at the end of a first semester with a 1.9 grade point. Doing too much at once, that was Dad's opinion. I'd shucked off his cautions and juggled a 17-hour class load, a fraternity pledge, a 40-hour job as a waiter, plus my needy hours with my girlfriend Jane. Graduating early from high school, I was still a month short of being old enough to leave home.

We fought during a night I tried to walk out on an argument. Our battle was over a curfew. I came in later than Mom wanted, and she knew I was having sex with that girlfriend. Mom might have worried I'd get my girlfriend pregnant while Jane was still in high school. Mom's story included a high school pregnancy that ended her classes. Dad had to get upset at me too, just to top her outrage.

"Where've you been?" He barked it out on the upslope to his anger.

"Seeing Jane." I headed toward the house's only bathroom with a shower. Downstairs was a cold-water sink and commode he'd installed. A beat up sofa sat in the rec room beside the bathroom.

He stepped in front of me. "You go downstairs."

"What the hell?"

"You want to be so separate from us, huh?" He looked over at Mom, frozen in silence. "You shouldn't be out that late. You've got school. Those grades can come up."

"Who are you to tell me?"

"Your father," he roared, rocking up on his toes, trying to stand taller than me. "You'll do what I say."

"I'm seeing her if I want."

"I don't care what you want," he said, coming up closer.

"I'm out of here." I pushed him away. He raised his fist and I backed off. When he lunged at me I swore this time it was going to be different. I reached for a knife on the kitchen counter.

"Oh, you want to play with knives, huh?" He was breathing hard with a shrill cry, almost like a laugh. He opened a drawer and took out a knife, not even looking at me. He hefted it.

"Hey," I said, "you can't…"

"Can't what? Tell you what to do? Do something when my kid pulls a knife on me?"

We scuffled in a tight circle on the yellow linoleum of the kitchen, a tract house room where two men would have to stand too close. I reached over and tipped a pot of water off the stove, splashing it onto the floor between us. It was something I'd seen in a Hawaii Five-O episode. Mom was shrieking behind Dad.

"Ronny, don't! Just go." Her eyes were wide. My chest pounded as Dad made his way across the water wearing his oxfords. He started to slip and I dropped my knife. I darted for the storm door, its hinges squawking, my Dad swearing, and Mom screaming at him to stop.

I didn't have a thought for where I'd go in the dark of March. I wanted to make a sweeping bit of drama, but my plan after my stagey exit was thin. I wore a yellow turtleneck sweater and corduroy pants, Converse high tops and no jacket. March is not a gentle month for Ohio weather, and I could see my breath in front of me as I arrived at the new Detwiler golf course. It was my first time to be there in the dark. The ground was wet, a dew thick on the fairways and slick on the greens. I trudged across it all without a care about the sod I was digging up with my Converse All-Stars.

The calm of the greens and fairways with the striking stars overhead slowed my pace. My heart stopped racing, and the ache in my hand from gripping that knife started to fall away. The wet and cold started to tamp down my mania.

When I got to the end of the course the wind started to pick up. I scanned the clubhouse and a tight bulwark of steel doors. I yanked on each one. Across the road, the yacht club was buttoned up and dark in a non-boating month. There was no shelter from the winds, not the cold ones inside me or the chilled north breeze off Maumee Bay. I crouched next to a storage unit, using it like a windbreak. My return in defeat, crawling back to more rage from Dad, was looking like a sure thing. He'd be awake, prowling his workshop in that basement, waiting to hear that storm door open. He might have even locked me out.

Security lights at the course tossed a glimmer on a fresh-built plywood shed for the rider mowers. I huddled next to the shed to get out of the wind and felt cold on the tip of my nose. The scent of new wood echoed my times as Dad's little workshop helper in that garage. He was good cutting wood on the weekends, measuring twice to cut once next to the workbench. The Shopsmith always roared loud enough that he had to shout to be heard over it. Somehow that shouting inside that one-car garage never scared me.

I flipped open the latch on the shed and pulled the door open. The space had just enough room between a mower and one edge of the shed. The smell of the cut grass on the mower mixed with the plywood's glue. I started to breathe naturally and spun the pinwheels in my mind, but ran out of ideas. Both of us went too far in that kitchen and we knew it, rushing to the brink of a fight that could leave scars. Maybe he'd be exhausted after that, like he often was after his rages. He had to go to bed by 11 because his work shift meant he'd be up before 6. I could steal back home. I slipped in as quietly as I could through the storm door he left unlocked for me. I went to bed with the smell of grass on me. No one spoke about the night, and a month later I left his house for good.

I had no grander ambition until that night except to better him at his own career, becoming an engineer with a degree. My nights in his workshop were an apprenticeship so I could achieve something to spark his praise. Maybe then he could make his way to love expressed out loud.

I SAW RIVERFRONT FOR THE FIRST TIME on the weekend before I entered the Army. In 1976 I took a game day trip to the town we called Cincy, treating myself with a splurge of freedom before shipping off to basic. Eighteen years later Nicky and I stood outside Riverfront's gates. The AstroTurf field inside was the same carpet from the Seventies, laid down over a blacktop base. It was a hard field, fast enough to make defense and base-running keys to success. Outside the field of turf that was colored green, the smell of something greener and organic rose up along Cincinnati's riverfront.

Although Riverfront baseball was carpeted, it charmed me because it was my cradle of baseball love. The stadium was brand new in 1970 when it launched the Big Red Machine. Two seasons of slugging, scoring, and legged out base hits built back-to-back Series titles. The field was less attractive. Riverfront was one of baseball's circular mistakes, ringed by four decks of concrete stands built in that era's massive, all-sport designs. Like the concrete ring in Pittsburgh at Three Rivers Stadium, Riverfront was not crafted for baseball, nothing like the Tiger Stadium we'd see on Friday in Detroit, the field where Dad's team won the 1968 Series. Despite playing in a soulless ashtray of a stadium, the Reds were my team and not my father's. Powerful WLW in Cincy carried the games to my radio. Loving the Reds instead of the Tigers was another article of my independence.

An usher tore our cardboard tickets at the gate and I peeled off five dollars for a program, the latest of a clutch of booklets we'd tote home. We descended from the concourse and stopped halfway down to survey the field.

I recalled little of that Saturday game I watched during my final weekend of baseball boyhood in Ohio. The Reds won that day, maybe. I sat up high with my girlfriend in the third deck. My memory of the stadium in '76 was so fuzzy that I drew a breath of surprise once Nicky and I neared the field.

There they stood, my Reds, warming up. At almost every stop of our schedule we'd see one of five teams: my Reds, Nicky's Cubs, my Rangers, his Cleveland Indians, or Dad's Tigers. Strictly by the luck of the schedule we'd already had a night of the Tigers at Kauffman. Riverfront had tugged us toward Ohio on the trip, instead of making a beeline for Chicago and Wrigley.

In Kansas City and in Arlington we arrived too late to see batting practice. But in Cincy the players were swinging when we first saw the field, major leaguers swatting balls to the fences or dropping some fly balls into the Green Level upper deck. Kids lined the rails behind home plate and the dugouts, waving programs, balls, and hats to autograph.

We edged our way down through the first level, well below our seats waiting upstairs in Section 219. An usher stopped us to demand a pass to get down to the rail. We had hard words for each other but he was in charge. Then he spotted Nicky and turned away. We hustled to a spot right behind the dugout.

We waved our fresh program, folded back to the blank scorecard stapled in the middle, but to no avail. Kids were shouting hard along the railings, calling out first names of every player who walked through the dugout and back into the clubhouse after taking BP. "Barry, Barry," they hollered, aiming for an autograph from Barry Larkin. He was one of a dozen Hall of Famers we'd see on our trip. Deion Sanders, speeding his way through major league ball and playing for the NFL the same year, waved and mugged.

But the players were not in a signing mood that evening. News about the impending player strike was building, a calamity Nicky and I hoped to outrun. Some of those guys on the field would be risking a third of their salary if they'd have to strike. Fans were restless about the players' demands for better pay. On a Monday where our $10 seats were one of the best bargains on the trip, there was still a wide gap between fan and player salaries. They'd have to settle the dispute soon. The prospect of a long strike was one more thing I could not control. Nicky went up to the Speed Pitch game booth to throw strikes as fast as 60. His strikes echoed the ones he threw in his championship game.

Cincinnati was the smallest market of all the towns we'd visit. The food prices matched the city's rank. Less than $4 got us a dog, peanuts and a soda. Cincy once had 38 breweries, but on that evening I was lucky to drink a beer not offered by Miller or Bud. It was many years before craft brewing or local beers in ballparks. A Heineken felt like a classy import. Nicky slurped a cola as we balanced our grey cardboard trays on our knees, spreading mustard on our fingers, shirttails and sleeves. We ate like savages with nary a napkin at hand.

Things were only a little neater down on the field. Knuckleballer Charlie Hough was starting for Florida, taking the mound at age 46 in the final season of a 24-year career. Any knuckler's odd pitches are just one toss from disaster, but when it works, the knuckleball can be unhittable. The Reds managed just five hits against him that evening. Hough was as interesting as promised, even getting called for a balk with his off-style delivery. He holds the record for single-game balks. In one four-inning start he got called for nine of them. His wild knuckleballs helped him finish in the Top 10 for hitting batters, too.

"You never know where it's going to go, with the knuckleball," I told Nicky. The night's baseball lesson was underway. The divorce denied me a voice in where Nicky went to school or what he studied, but class was in session at Riverfront. Baseball can be a means to learn about many things, subjects such as chance or perceptions. Knuckleballers are the rarest elements in the periodic table of pitchers. I had to prove that with a statistic. "Only four pitchers out of more than 300 are throwing a knuckler this year."

Nicky shifted in his seat and marked down another strike. Ballgames get slow. The scorebook always gave us something to do while we watched, waiting for something to happen. Baseball is best when things are close and the game slows down, everyone waiting for a mistake like a home run pitch or some batter fanning on a bases-loaded strikeout. I chose a baseball trip because of the time to talk that's built into every game.

Nicky gave me questions to make the talk easier. "So what's a knuckleball got to do with a balk?"

"When you commit a balk, you wind up and come to the belt, then change your mind and start again," I said.

"The belt?"

"Literally, the belt, the one they're wearing. It's called 'coming set.' Knuckleballers have an unusual motion, different delivery." I popped the last bite of the $1.50 dog in my mouth. "Umps don't see knucklers much, so they don't see balks, either."

"But we might? Where do I put it in the scorebook?"

"Right at the bottom of the pitching box. See?"

He watched Hough. "Balk!" he hollered. It took a few innings, but a balk did appear. It would be the only one we'd see in more than 90 innings of baseball, one of the things fans always claim to see and holler because the ump's missed it.

"Balk!" Nicky put down his cola and reached for another fry.

The chanting rose up around us. "Yeah ump, balk."

"He's getting away with another one there," I said. "Ol' Charley Hough, king of the knucklers."

"Slow-speed junk he's pitching, huh?"

We watched his pitches baffle one Red after another. Things got rocky for Charlie in the sixth, though. One Reds outfielder cleared the fence in left with a homer. On the very next at bat, Sanders slapped Hough's too-slow knuckler with that special crack of the bat. The crowd's roar rose up around the ball. "You know," I said, "a home run sometimes sounds different. He's got good junk, but not good enough, it seems," I said.

"Yeah, serving up the long-ball," he said. We watched the fly drop into the stands beyond the right field.

"That'll be the end of Charlie," I said.

"Because he's a knuckler," Nicky replied.

We turned to each other to slap a high-five, and then I added a Three Stooges catcall. "Nyuk, nyuk, nyuk."

"Wooo-woo-woo-woo-woo," he said back. The Stooges were our guy thing. It was like dancing, those times when we'd make a joke together, slathering a comic bit onto a moment we understood as men, one very young and one not so young anymore. At age 46, Hough had just one more inning left in his career. A balk is the sin of changing your mind on a pitch. I'd followed through with my dream of coming back, and maybe I had Riverfront in my Sports Shots vision. I brought a boy who'd pitched for a save in a Little League title game, too.

AAA GUIDEBOOKS DO NOT HAVE CATEGORIES for the Worst Parts of Town in their lodging listings, but the Days Inn we'd booked had definitely seen better days. We made our way to our room by picking out our steps carefully, not looking aside as we walked through clutches of people milling around one room's open door, and farther down, another room. People were living in that Days Inn, not visiting. I'd gone too low budget on my reservations.

In the middle of the night came the sounds of a fight, the yelling in that vivid tone that beers will bring on. We woke up and I turned on the light. We had the light to chase off the sound of those angry voices. I started to get angry myself for putting us in such a flea-trap of a flophouse. Then the voices got comic.

"I told you, ya shit. I don't know where you put that damn key."

"Didn't give it to me. No you didn't.

"Well then search me if you want."

"Ain't the police. I ain't searching you."

Nicky started to giggle. "It's like Cops," he said. "Like we're on TV."

" 'Bad boys, bad boys, whatcha gonna do?' " I sang softly.

" 'Whatcha gonna do when they come for you?' " Nicky giggled back.

The voice outside barked again. "Let's look," Nicky said, creeping to the window's vinyl drapes. I followed him, staying close behind, and just before we arrived at the window, there was a thump and a bang on our door.

"Not there, asshole. That's not even our room."

My heart was pounding, but I took a step closer to Nicky and eked out a smile. He had heard angry voices in the nights before this one, those fights I waged with his mom. But at the Days Inn, the loud voices didn't belong to anybody in the family. Just as he peeked between the curtains, a sound like a baseball bat hitting a home run rang out next door. We raced back to our beds, turned on the TV loud and found something that involved explosions.

"Sorry about that," I said during a commercial.

"About what?" His eyes didn't leave the screen.

"The room. This place."

"It's okay. I'm not scared."

He fell asleep sitting up against his pillows on the bed. The voices from next door were gone. I turned out the light on the stand between our beds, and then the TV. I looked over at him sleeping just before I dowsed the light. Bedtimes were the moments I hadn't had enough of since I'd left his house. I started to add them up, those overnights, and I got to a number like 274 before I fell asleep.

THE NEXT MORNING WE HAULED OUR DUFFEL BAGS down to the lobby, moving in the funeral-home quiet of the early morning after a drunk-loud night. We passed by the steel door of the room next to ours and saw that a massive dent had chipped away some of the thick white paint. Anger passed over our door last night. We didn't balk as we completed our move to evacuate from the Days Inn. No point in complaining about a hotel we'd never stay at again.

The toughest moments of parenting are when it's a spectator sport. My two weeks of wandering included plenty of planned time as a spectator, the nine games of baseball we'd watch together. But I was watching myself try to be a full-time father during the trip, too. It seemed like an easy endeavor at first. Who couldn't enjoy a couple of weeks of summertime ballgames?

There was more to see than baseball, though. I'd just eased us out of low-rent Cincinnati and didn't say a word about how scared I was that something dangerous might spoil the trip. I wanted to be perfect for two weeks, dodging all risks, my not-on-my-watch ideal of a divorced parent.

After our long Cincinnati night I pulled onto the Interstate happy, looking at the graffiti on the side of the I-75 on-ramp.

"Like we're leaving the scene of the crime," I said to Nicky.

"Bad town," he said.

"Yeah, bad town. Bad!" Like scolding a dog.

"Nah. But a bad hotel."

"Bad-ass."

He giggled, and I tried not to blame myself so much.

"So much for the accuracy of a AAA guidebook. Onward to a nicer place."

"Dad, will the next place have a steel door, too?"

I looked across the seat and spied him smiling. "Well, it is Cleveland." I could joke because safety surrounded us in the morning's light, sunny and clear on a mid-July day.

I gave little thought to whether Nicky's mom would want to see a card from him. And I told myself that a long distance call to her was going to cost money, and I was spending enough already. I was being cheap, and it would cost me. I parried her thrusts of control over his schedule with my vacation disregard.

NOBODY DRIVES IN A STRAIGHT LINE TO CLEVELAND, do they? It would have been all of 271 miles by the Triptik's tally, maybe four hours of burning $1.12 a gallon gas. I turned us away from I-71 and the straightest route, then past Dayton, then toward the little town of Wapakoneta.

"Hey, want to see a hero's hometown?"

He lolled about, slouched against the door, playing Game Boy on the blue cloth seat. "Huh?"

"From when I was your age. An astronaut."

"I guess."

"Neil Armstrong. Moon landing?"

"Yeah." He sat up and grabbed the Ohio guidebook. "Says in here there's a museum."

I played the role of a surprised dad. "Really?"

The heroes we called spacemen were as obvious as the cornfields unfolding on the Ohio horizon. I was unsure how I could share with Nicky everything the astronauts meant when I was his age. Those earnest men in short haircuts were rock stars for straight arrows like my parents; we grew up in groovy Sixties glory. In the final year of that decade our family took a summer road vacation while the Apollo 11 mission got underway. The family listened on AM in the car where the launch was playing on every channel. Once we got home, in our downstairs playroom I slipped the stories from the vacation newspapers into my three-ring binder with *Toledo Blade* clippings about the Apollo missions.

Any grade school boy of that time would track heroes. I wanted to tell Nicky how my house felt during the evening just three nights after radio had buzzed with the launch. Men were orbiting the moon.

I'd never told him my story of that night in July. And wasn't that the point of these two weeks with him? He could learn who I was and some of who my dad had been to me, if I could only tell him. If nothing else, we could talk so he wouldn't get quite as bored riding all those miles.

"Want to hear a story about that night?"

"Which night?"

"The moon landing."

"How old were you, dad?"

I steered us off the Interstate, slowing at the Wapakoneta exit. "Sort of your age."

"What was so special about it?"

"We'd waited a long time. Years."

"Kinda like the Cubs winning, hah."

"Not that long. But it was, well…" I looked over the string of farmhouses that dotted the low hills. "That night your granddad was happy," I began, giving him the headline. "We all were happy, inside those walls and in front of that TV."

"Like a shuttle launch, right?"

"Yeah, a lot like that. Everything stopped that night, though. Nobody was doing anything anywhere but watching the landing on the TV. A console on the floor, like the one in your house." I flashed on that house as the one where we lived and played together before the divorce. "That night it was like when you and me used to watch TV sitting on the floor right in front of it."

"Television!" He said it like Homer did in the Simpsons parody of *The Shining*, picking up the Jack Nicholson routine. "Teacher. Mother. Secret lover."

"Urge to kill," I said, slipping in the line like a call and response in church, "fading, fading."

"Rising," he said.

"Fading, fading. Gone." We exhaled together with a sigh just like in the cartoon. We knew our lines together.

The astronauts' stars were fading while Nicky and I walked through Armstrong's museum in Wapakoneta. I had my own museum of Nicky back at home, stocked with kindergarten projects like baby food jars holding colored sand. The drawings of tanks and police cars were growing ever more detailed since the divorce. Each was a talisman to remind me of his love, especially on days he was away. Like the moon rocks in the museum trying to represent a celestial body, Nicky's artwork didn't stand in well for everyday fatherhood. But we claimed our inner space together during our tour of that outer space museum.

Dad's space was his inner sanctum basement workshop. Just beyond the wall where he hung his guns, I filled those astronaut scrapbooks. The playroom floor didn't have tile like in the rec room. The concrete was cold in the winters but cool in the summer afternoons. The stairs conducted the sound of family.

The sound of feet on the metal runner of each step gave away whoever was on the stairs. Dad's tread was different than Mom's. Hers meant the laundry was starting up, cleaning the dirty clothes already delivered down a chute from the bathroom upstairs. Dad's footsteps could mean more than one thing. A reason for me to play quieter, if he was tired. Or a time to go ask him questions, so he could warm to me as he showed off what he knew. I liked him happy and wished for those not-tired footsteps, crisper than the ones on the nights he came home sullen. Downstairs Dad might create recordings with his stereo and tape decks, making the predecessors of playlists, or just spin Buck Owens records, shuffling around the workshop I thought of as his playroom.

Beside his workbench he'd mounted sat a radio on a shelf. The Bandcaster had a fine-tuning dial, five shortwave bands for foreign stations, plus AM for US and Canadian stations. On the floor underneath the radio sat the one grownup toy we could share with him. Underneath that radio a wooden box with grey latches held a tube-tester, more than a dozen sockets and a pair of meters for vacuum tubes. "Dad, can I test your tubes?" He'd hand over a cardboard box with the same twenty tubes. I could do my electronics right alongside him.

His sanctuary had scripture, too. There was paper to balance all of the tools and tech, sets of Time-Life books about stars and electrical sourcebooks of schematics for building things. Across the room, a metal filing cabinet usually had one drawer pulled open so the electronics magazines stacked inside could reveal their spines but not their covers. On the wall that was lined with pegboard he'd cut out a square window just the size of an album cover. It was a projector window. Dad inserted two layers of glass to shield the rec room from the sound of the projector. Its panes had to remain polished perfectly clean for a movie to be shown through. Dad had carved a professional projection room out of the space in his workshop.

He'd stand in that workshop and run the movies, reliving his wartime duty of naval station projectionist. The projectors splashed out the soundless family movies shot in Super 8. Sitting in the rec room I would glance back at Dad through the window. His glasses always slid down his nose. On the nights without movies he'd also be in that workshop. He would tell us to knock if we wanted to come in. I sometimes preferred observing him through that window.

One night I knocked on the door and Dad slid the bolt open. I stepped in quickly before he changed his mind or asked what I wanted. There had to be something he was locking away in there. As I pushed past him, my head not yet tall enough to reach his shoulder, he cracked off a line. "So boy, what's the rush? You looking for something you lost in here?"

"Looking for you. You lock yourself in here."

He put down his soldering gun and pushed his glasses back up his nose. "So? It's my own damn space. You kids have the rest of the damn house. I get one room."

"We only have the playroom." I watched his face to see if I'd set him off, hoping not.

"You kids gripe about anything, don't ya?"

"I'm not griping. I'm just saying. You get your room." I looked away from him and toward the door. "We don't get to see you when that's closed."

"This isn't easy shit here, boy. I gotta have quiet from the racket, to focus. Or I'll fuck something up. You don't want that, do you?"

Making something perfect was always an excuse for not talking. I adored perfect the way he and Mom taught me. Perfect meant best. In a family with three kids in the house, being best meant being loved the most. But now that I was inside the door and he hadn't yelled yet, I said what I was thinking.

"You build cool stuff in here, I know."

"Damn right." He stuck a hand into his trouser pocket and fiddled with coins in there.

"Maybe you build something else at the same time." I took my shot. "Like you're building up space. Space away from us."

"From who?"

"From me. From Bob."

"You're talking like you wanna be in here with me. Sometimes it doesn't work like that."

"Why not?"

He plugged in a smaller red soldering gun, pulling its trigger to check it was delivering heat. He eyed the little light that clicked on just beneath the gun's wand. "One man, one bench, son. What my dad taught me. Now this damn solder joint's probably cold."

A cold solder joint. A thing that made you start over because it wouldn't pass electricity, something imperfect. Something that would make Dad swear. He'd learned that pretty well in the Navy, he said. While he focused on the bench he asked what was the point of my jabbering.

"What about the window you cut out of the wall? You want to see us, but still hide out."

He set down the gun and looked at me quick. "The window's for the projector. You know that."

I backed away a step. "This lock, though." I fingered the door latch. "The lock isn't like the window. This keeps us out."

"And the other one lets me see." He moved to grab the door and ease me out as he closed it. "So I can watch you." He caught himself and added, "I can watch over you."

Across the thousands of miles of our trip I was seeking the difference between a dad's surveillance and loving protection. Being with Nicky every day, just the two of us, was transporting me from observing to loving. Ahead of us lay Cleveland, the last city between us and my boyhood hometown where that house and its basement still stood.

A BREAK AT THE JAKE
Rangers vs. Indians
Jacobs Field, Cleveland
Tuesday, July 19

Cleveland had a reputation as a punch line all my life. So did my hometown of Toledo. Our family built a retort by saying at least we weren't Cleveland. On the afternoon that Nicky and I drove into that city, I wanted it to be a respite from the road and the uncertainties of travel. People vacation to see new things, I told myself. I wanted to see Cleveland anew, a place of comfort and safety.

The city was not a mystery to enter, the exit off the Interstate as simple as finding a drawbridge at a castle. Nicky read hotel directions to me as I maneuvered the Sunbird through downtown streets that surprised me with their bustle.

"Left on 14th," he said.

"Coming up," I said, then stole a glance at him holding the AAA Ohio map. The good city maps were still on the big paper, not the Triptik. "So then what?"

"Long way, and then a left."

"Onto?"

"Euclid. I mean, Superior. No, Euclid."

"And from there?" I heard my voice take on the rising tone of my dad's. I was wary of snapping a tripwire like Dad's, so I checked myself. Nicky wouldn't hear that from me. "I mean, I don't wanna miss the hotel."

"I think we turn right again, onto 12th."

"12th, 14th. Okay then. You have your breakout bag packed?"

"Sure, even with my music."

"Your Stone Temple Pilots," I said, "and hey, here they are," reaching for the radio knob. With our top down, so I could see the street signs easier, the rock of 102.3 spilled out of the convertible speakers and into the Cleveland summertime. The July air was balmy like bathwater on a Saturday night.

We tooled down two blocks of Euclid like we owned a building there. I wasn't sore from sitting on the drive, or blinking back sleep this time. The sun's heat was held back by a cool wind from Lake Erie blowing through my hair. Nicky's too, because he took his Cubs ball cap off. We were at the home of his Indians. I expected little from our hotel room in midtown, since the memory of our flea-trap in Cincy was still raw.

A sign for valet parking swung up on the right when we pulled into the hotel's driveway. The parking garage lay underneath what I might call a skyscraper when I was Nicky's age. Black with tinted windows, the building roared all the way up 35 stories. If there was an opposite to Cincy's dump of a hotel, this was it.

"You wanna be sure you have your toothbrush."

"Aw dad, do I have to?" He giggled. "We could make garbage angels in the room." Another Simpsons joke, this time about Bart's dad being so lax that the trash piled up in the house and they did their parody of snow angels.

"Boy," I said, taking on Homer's voice, "I don't think we'll be in there long enough to trash up the place that much."

"Hey, I could brush my teeth with Coke."

"Just be sure your mother doesn't find out, boy."

We were downtown in the upscale blocks, not in some gully alongside an old freeway like in Cincy. In the driveway a red-coated teenager, looking fresh out of high school, opened our door. "Welcome to the Radisson."

I gave him a thank-you in the tone I polished up during my business trips. After the Cincinnati Days Inn with its steel door, we felt like kings returned to our palace. This was our first hotel where valet was available. I peeled off a few singles to tip and we snatched up our duffels, because I wanted to avoid the bag tip inside. More economy. The boy parking our car asked if I was sure I wanted to leave the Sunbird's top down. I raised our roof. Being in a downtown Cleveland hotel, I figured the town to be rough.

Nicky leaned over as he grabbed his backpack and looked at the valet. "Cool." He stood at the curb and watched him drive off.

I splashed out his nickname for the trip, an homage to a pair of Nicky's escaped pet rabbits. "The Flying Rabbit Tour, m'boy. Nothing but the best."

"Tonight, anyway. No cops."

I dropped into my Bullwinkle Moose voice. "No, this time for sure!" Nicky crinkled his nose at this. "C'mon, Bullwinkle? Moose and Squirrel," I added in the voice of Boris Badenov.

"Sure, Dad. Just let me get the "Not Insane" stamp for your hand." Another Simpsons reference to the episode where Homer gets thrown into an asylum. There was a flicker of pushback in me, triggered from Dad's stays in the psych ward before he died. The hospital wasn't funny then. It was a place where Dad didn't get better. But the Simpsons had made a mental ward comic. Dark comedy. Dad might have approved.

Inside the hotel, the lobby floor was marble and the entrance had a revolving door that swished with its sweeps. The front desk was a gold-flecked altar where beaming clerks stood behind the blond stone. After getting our mini-bar key at check-in, I could see that our hotels up to then had been low-grade bargains. Simple taste had led me to someplace special this time, somehow. Dad would say we caught a break.

We got real keys, brass with big plastic tabs suited for any Sixties apartment. It began to add up, all these pieces of a higher caliber. The elevator did not rattle, and carpets lined the halls with red plush, their ample nap showing they'd just been vacuumed.

Inside the room, black leather covered a couch and ran along a few walls, like the one next to a wet bar. Beside the bar there was a second room. We toured the rooms and laughed, yammering about the crystal lights, the gauzy sheers between curtains and a window with a nice view, the pair of TVs for just one room. We unpacked, slipping our wrinkled clothes into dressers that slid out clean and quiet.

"Whoa, cool," Nicky said. "Dad, you rock."

It's what every dad wants to hear from a child. The notes sang out. Dad and son, love said out loud, the combination I craved as a boy. To Nicky's words that I lived to hear, I could only reply, "Yeah, something special here. I suspect this was more than just a hotel, and not very long ago."

The couch became a pullout bed in the living room, and the windows went from floor to ceiling. I let myself sink into a padded leather chair and threw my feet onto an ottoman. A town that I thought was down on its luck was treating us right, and I could feel a breath wriggle out of me in a slow sigh. Not just comfort here. Peace.

"Too bad we have to go to a game," Nicky said.

"Very nice. But we have these tickets, you know. Seats in The Jake. Sold out, I'm sure." Brand new, the ballpark already had a reputation for a hot night. And the team was good, too. Baseball was on the rise in Cleveland at last.

"Oh, I'm down for that Indians baseball," he said. "We're gonna take down your Rangers."

My obsession with scheduling was paying off. It was one of three games where our teams faced off. "Maybe they win. Maybe not." I endured that loss in Texas. Another wouldn't be fun.

"How about a bet then?" He fished into his jeans and pulled out a few wrinkled dollars. "Just enough for Dippin' Dots."

I took his money and matched it with mine. "It's the Ice Cream of the Future, you know."

"Okay, loser buys the Dots. And it's gonna be you."

THE ROOM REPRESENTED THE CLEVELAND THE TOWN wanted to become. The more I looked it over, the easier I understood the nature of the surprise. This had been an apartment building, perhaps luxury in its day, reclaimed from a faded Cleveland that once featured a river that once caught fire from its pollution, rusting industry, and an elderly sports stadium called the Mistake by the Lake. Our hotel wasn't priced like a high-toned address—I never would have picked someplace in that tier. This was a find, a $103 steal, good luck wearing good looks. That hotel was just as reborn as Cleveland's baseball and the sparkling new toothbrush-on-end-shaped lights down at Jacobs Field. We could get there with a walk down the streets, the bellman told us at the door.

"Really?"

"Oh yes sir. It's very safe. We're retaking the downtown, you know."

After a couple of blocks down East Ninth, Nicky wanted to know what all that retaking was about. "Probably a rough place, not so long ago," I said.

"Before they built the new park."

"It sure looks like it." The street was busy as the sun began to set over the lakeside, the sidewalks alive with fans wearing Indians gear. Some were laughing like they'd come out of the little taverns along the way. Jacobs Field's lights started to apply their glow to the skyline around us. It was a holiday from my worry, a night to savor a surprise of "The Comeback City," as it was tagged in the Rand McNally atlas.

For the first time on the trip we walked along downtown streets to a game. The leather furniture and the valet and the restaurants with chalkboards and outside seating were a sign. Not all of our trip's surprises were going to trigger my anxiety. This was a place to write home about. There would be postcards in the ballpark's gift shop. Cleveland, that punch line like my hometown Toledo, had developed some surprises. I didn't know everything about this place, although I grew up within a two-hour drive and believed I did. The good luck was a glimpse at the idea that unplanned moments could carry special charms.

We lifted our pace once we crossed Euclid Avenue, looking over at a diner that had a chalkboard with Walleye Special scrawled on it. A real Ohio fish, that one. Then we passed a restaurant adding a deck, not quite finished and carrying the scent of sawdust in the air. I smiled inside and out. Sawdust surrounded my dad on the days that I loved him easily enough to kiss him.

THAT GARAGE WAS DAD'S SATURDAY EMPIRE, once he began to get his days off on weekends instead of mid-week. There were many things in his life he could not control, but the garage's array of metal and wood let him exercise his powers of absolute domain.

Along the planks of one garage wall three names were stenciled, mine, Bob's, and my sister Tina's. In red spray-painted letters, each name was centered in a panel between the exposed studs of the wall. His tidy love notes, they were, organizing us over a thick plywood toy box he built underneath the names. Inside the box, though, there were no dividers, so our toys lived in a jumble. There were arguments at first, but after a while we learned it didn't matter. Dad's appearance of organization was the most important part of his toy chest scheme, putting things out of sight to establish order.

On the other side of the garage the Shopsmith hovered on its four metal

legs. Each leg had a wheel that could be locked down, and upon those legs sat a table saw, a drill press, a router and lathe, a band saw, a sander, all powered by the same electrical engine. On many Saturday mornings it commanded the center of the one-car garage, but on weeknights it idled beside the Plymouth Fury. Although that car was wide like a Seventies classic, Dad always parked it cleanly, never nearing the leviathan of the Shopsmith. He parked the Fury with precision without any help of painted lines on the floor or a tennis ball dangling off a cord from the ceiling. The Fury was the biggest sedan ever to park in the garage, but its back bumper never failed to be tucked inside the door.

A radio he mounted on the garage workbench had two sets of speakers, one inside and a second pair mounted on the outside wall of the garage. Dad reclaimed the outside speakers from a drive-in movie, buying them from Toledo's surplus electronics store Warren Radio. He mounted them on either side of the garage door, lined up with the precision of a drill team. A knob beside the radio routed the music—songs from CKLW, the Big 8— either through the radio's workbench speakers, those outside, or both. Dad wired it all.

The tools hung on pegboard with handles he'd painted green, covering up the previous generation of orange. He took them on after his dad died.

Only the most-used tools, the hacksaws, showed any evidence of their orange-handled heritage. His vise mounted on the end of the bench was brushed clean and oiled, the cloying scent of 3-in-1 Oil hovering around the aroma of just-cut lumber.

While I'd stand alongside him he'd cut lumber, a hobby carpenter who could build rough furniture and cabinets, or cut paneling for the basement walls. Dad let me hold the loose end of the wood he was cutting, giving in after he'd told me for a half-hour to stay back from the power saws.

He worked in trousers no matter what the season. "Nobody builds in Bermuda shorts, Ronny. A man wears pants."

The change rolled around in the pockets of the beige workingman's trousers, pants with the same belt he'd wear to his job with dress pants. He moved between the workbench and the Shopsmith back and forth like a dancer, measuring and drawing lines across two-by-fours with the pencil he'd tuck behind his ear while he cut. Up and down the street, the sounds of such garage enterprise filled backyards on Saturdays after the good cartoons were over. I loved the sawdust part of him.

He was at his best while he worked in front of us, especially if it was a task that had little at stake. When he'd repair something in that garage, the lightning strike of his anger could bolt out at some object that defied a tool. A slipped screwdriver or a bent nail head would uncork a spume of swearing, from the garden-variety goddammit to the nuclear warhead of motherfucker, with sonofabitch as a ready bridge. The anger wasn't lashed at my brother or me in those moments of high drama. We'd back away a little, but he'd cool down and retake control with a little lecture.

"Now this Phillips head is stripped out, so we use the channel locks to get that damn thing out of the wood," he explained.

"Yeah. I see."

"And you tighten it all with this screw on the bottom handle of the vise grip here." He spun the tiny wheel. "See?"

"Great, Dad."

"You'll probably do this when you've got boys, too."

"I sure hope so."

"Just don't have 'em too early," he said as he pushed his hair back. "Wait awhile."

"Okay." I did the math while I watched him. He was 41 during that summer of '68 in the garage, old enough to be a hero to me on that day. I felt warmth in my gut while I got close to him and held the end of the board he was cutting.

"Just loose now. Don't force it. I'm cutting. You're holding."

"Sure, Dad."

I WANTED TO BE A SAWDUST DAD FOR NICKY, not a crazy blade. Throughout our trip I fed him whatever he wanted to eat. We never passed a McDonald's around lunch or supper without considering it.

"The fries," he'd say. "You know you want the fries, Dad."

"Then we can get you a Happy Meal." Although I took the risk of teasing him, it was not a serious gamble.

"No Dad, you'll get the Happy Meal. I'm having a Quarter Pounder."

"With cheese."

McDonald's didn't always rule our diet. In southern Ohio we got White Castle for lunch. A bag of tiny burgers that we'd call sliders years later. And fries, of course. At 37, I could still eat fries every day and keep my pants buttoned in the weeks afterward. The real food was at the ballpark every game night. No Mickey D's meal with a pink plastic toy travel cup. Most nights our suppertime plastic was team souvenir soda cups and mini-helmets of soft-serve ice cream.

The Indians were one of Nick's two teams, and 1994 was a good season to see them. After years of decay, the team was contending. Jacobs Field was named after the club's owner in that era before corporate-named parks. Opened in the same year as the Rangers' new park, the Jake felt more finished, somehow. The grass was also new at the Rangers' park, but in Cleveland the new grass was lush from the lakeside rains, unlike the infield grass struggling in the Texas heat. The Jake's concourses sparkled like our starry smiles. We were up in Row U of an outfield section and happy to have any seats in a sellout crowd. We stood down by the rail for BP and warm-ups. Indians fielders like the speedster Kenny Lofton and the slugger Jim Thome loosened up with tosses between them, throwing and catching right in front of us. The Indians were one of Nicky's teams during the days when he memorized lineups and pitching rotations. He gazed at players as if they were gods. Our outfield row would be a pew of his church.

We'd moved down during batting practice next to the first base line. The green edge of the grass ran in front of us, just a couple of strides away.

"Close enough to see the crushed granite in the dirt," I said.

"What a weird color," he said, eyeing the gray sand along the edges of the infield. The Jake had the only grey infield dirt in the majors, an element of the Ohio River's mud.

We sang along to the National Anthem standing on the concourse instead of hurrying to our seats. We were together on a Tuesday, a weeknight we might only share in Texas if it was on a holiday visit. On the way to our seats we stopped to stare at the outfield lights. They ran vertically up massive poles, not fanned out across the top like most ballpark lights. The odd shape made them seem alive somehow, infused with electricity.

We rolled our program absent-mindedly while we watched the game, swapping the Bibb Falk back and forth. It was a packed house. The scalpers outside the gates helped create that, a string of sellouts in that first season that paraded the first new sports venue in Cleveland. 1994 was the opening salvo of the long-ball era. Teams slugged their way to championships. For the first time, we were at a ballpark watching our teams battle one another.

The Indians hammered Rangers pitcher Hector Fajardo early, clubbing him for four runs in the first. It was a replay of the trip's opening night. Things were starting out badly as Fajardo limped through the first five innings until once again he faced Albert Belle, the Indians' home-run king. Belle had just been found guilty of cheating with an illegal bat. The bats he used that year had illegal cork centers in their barrels, making them easier to swing. He'd posted an appeal, however, so he was on the field before us.

"Mr. Albert Belle," Nicky crowed as Belle left the on-deck circle. The crowd roared its approval for its outlaw star. As the rumors had swelled, Belle had hidden his corked bats in the clubhouse above the ceiling panels.

"Yeah, yeah," I said, like any fan whose team was already down 6-1. "Who couldn't hit all those homers with that bat?"

"Nobody's proved it yet." He grinned. "Just watch."

"He'll have to hit one for real, now that his bat's legal. We're gonna sit him down with a strikeout."

The back and forth between us was as much fun as anything down on that gentle grass. Nicky looked at me and howled, "Belle!" alongside 41,743 other fans. A few of us rooted for the Rangers. Belle worked to a full count in a classic baseball back-and-forth, fouling off pitches to keep himself alive, then drove a ball deep into the centerfield stands. When the dinger dropped to our right, it was the fourth Indians homer of the night. The cheers raked through the park.

"How about that!" Nicky screamed. My team absorbed a 12-3 loss and Nicky collected his bet. He tucked away the money instead of buying Dippin' Dots.

BACK IN OUR LEATHER-CLAD HOTEL ROOM I turned on the TV in our suite. The boob tube, as Dad enjoyed calling it, was turned to Channel 8, WJW, biggest of the local stations. Toledo's airwaves had no Channel 8, but WJW was a place Dad might have moved up to. Cleveland was a bigger place than Toledo to us. He'd mocked the chance to move us all to Cleveland. I learned about it one day when the antenna on our roof brought in the mystery of Channel 8.

"Hey, it's Eight," I said, running to the antenna control box atop the TV set.

"You went too far," Dad said. "Seven is Detroit."

"I know, but it's Cleveland. Ever think of working there, Dad?"

His face clouded. "Even if they did ask me, I'd have said no. Not worth it."

"They wouldn't pay you enough?"

"Not enough to move all of you kids, and your mom. Sell the house, criminy, all of that." He flexed his hands and rubbed them. "Besides, they weren't as good as they thought they were." The same company that owned his station owned Channel 8, but I didn't know that.

"So then, you like Channel 13 better?" He was talking and it made me bold. I asked my question knowing his answer, the stain he put on his station.

"Those bastards. I gave them everything I had. I was there before the place was even finished."

I knew this mantra. "Wires everywhere, right?"

"Damn right. I built that place. You saw when we went down there. I know that place like the back of my hand, dammit."

He might have cursed it because he got comfortable in the safety and routine. Toledo became a place with little risk. Cleveland was bigger, maybe better. It had a pro baseball team. Toledo was as high as he'd climb while taking us along. If he'd been without kids, a wife, a mortgage in the suburbs, he might have risen to Cleveland. Legend had it that Dad got a shot at working in New York at a network. Cleveland's reclaimed marvels, spooled out along Lakeshore Boulevard outside our hotel window, were out of Dad's reach. Grabbing them might have given us all a poke.

I looked in on Nicky while he slept in his bed on the other side of the suite. I never took a job anywhere but Austin once he was born. I didn't want a poke, either. The distance between our houses in Austin was already greater than I wanted. I couldn't bring him along to any new city if I'd changed jobs. My dad couldn't either—his reasons having as much to do with his kids as mine did with Nicky.

Dad taught me an electrical circuit must be grounded to operate safely. He was grounded in Toledo with kids who he couldn't get to know better. I was grounded in Austin with a son I wanted to know more. I was connecting, despite my anxiety about being imperfect at it. I congratulated myself on the upgrade. Our road trip time together was completing our circuit.

LOVE ON THE POINT
Travel Day
Wednesday, July 20

Cities of my home state delivered a creaking park of champions in Cincinnati, then our Cleveland evening in a park as new as a '94 penny. I had no Cleveland memories because we never got that far on family road trips. Going further was my game plan with Nicky.

On our third day in Ohio I drove toward a much older, happy memory to give my son. We pushed away from Cleveland on the Ohio Turnpike to Cedar Point, a mecca of roller coasters and the heartland of my summer joy. I learned that the only thing that could ever spoil Cedar Point was rain. Whenever Dad took us, the trip was as guaranteed as Christmas to have no earthquakes of anger. You had to pay to have your fun at Cedar Point, Dad figured, and so fun was all you should have. Not many days had that kind of assurance from him. I adored the anticipation of it. On the eve of every trip it was hard to get to sleep, like Christmas in July.

By that morning after our Cleveland game, Cheetos and Doritos and abandoned fries dotted the blue-gray carpet and the vinyl valleys of the Sunbird's floor. The snacks were ground-in, the air ripe with the scent of Dr. Pepper, gum of fruity varieties, and malted milk balls gone missing in the car's crannies. The cloth seats were already damp from the day's muggy air. Stacked between the seats, resting on the case of CDs, the Triptik fluttered in the breeze while we drove. The AAA map was folded back to reveal the Ohio Turnpike route. I glanced at our manila toll ticket with its list of exits. They were like cast members from a beloved movie, the names I knew from memory when we drove eastbound from Toledo to the park: Perrysburg, Wyandot, Elmore, Port Clinton, and finally Norwalk. But I was traveling from the east toward Cedar Point for the first time. That cast of turnpike exits running from the east toward Cedar Point was new.

Guitar with heavy bass and wailing lyrics rose out of the speakers mounted in the Sunbird's doors, pouring across our dusty dashboard. It was rock that the lakeshore winds could not overpower. The sun that came through that windshield also pounded on the cloth convertible top, while the highway breeze rumbled under the roof's ribs. The wind gathered itself against the car's porthole of a rear window.

Tennis shoes that were still tied but kicked off littered the floor in front of Nicky's seat. The green mileage signs counted down the distance to Marblehead, Sandusky and Toledo beyond. Across the back seat and on the floor behind our bucket seats, the programs from Cleveland, Cincinnati, Kansas City, and Texas, along with his *Goosebumps* paperbacks, fluttered in whatever summer wind could catch them.

The sky turned bluer as we followed the highway heading west. It was our first day to drive in that direction after five days heading east and north. The morning's sun was behind us for the first time. The light bounced again onto the silver letters of Sunbird stamped on the glove box door. No rain today.

"Dad, can we can ride there all day?"

"Just like Six Flags." I shifted into the novelty of fifth and raised my voice while the throaty engine roar crept into our cockpit. "Until they close up and chase us out."

"The biggest is the Magnum, right?"

"For this year, anyway. They put up new coasters all the time. Spend millions." I heard myself sound like an investor's brochure for the park that had been on the Ohio shore for over a century. At Cedar Point we'd meet Bob, plus Tina and her three girls, giving us four kids on hand from age 6 to 11. The kids would span the same ages as when I went with my family at Nicky's age.

"I've been wanting to take you here for a long time," I said.

"Me too."

"You want to take me?"

"Sure. That's what's happening, Dad. You wouldn't be going if it weren't for me."

I looked over at him and plucked the turnpike ticket from under his visor. I put it in his hands. "You'll know the way if you've got that. It's the Number 7 exit, Sandusky Norwalk."

"It doesn't say Cedar Point?"

"Not necessary. Not if you grew up here, at least."

I was showing him the way, and he saw that day's meaning. My family used to go to the park on Wednesdays, one of Dad's mid-week days off. Wednesday was away from the weekend prices and the longer lines in Ohio's steamy summer afternoons.

IN THE SIXTIES, CEDAR POINT WAS ANNOUNCED ON BILLBOARDS for 20 miles before we'd close in. It brought my family together—a roller coaster, carousel, and sky ride-rich road trip. Going in the middle of the week was our consolation for Dad's irregular work schedule. We had one Cedar Point day each year. It was the only day I'd ever cross a causeway, the slender, rock-lined road to the park that spanned a finger of Lake Erie to the point. We lived in Point Place growing up, bordered by the Ottawa River and Maumee Bay. The waters around Cedar Point felt bigger. This was no bay or river. This was a Great Lake. We'd pay a causeway toll on the way in, one more excruciating stop before getting there.

Dad would fork over three 10-dollar bills at the ticket window to get everybody into the park. As he'd walk off and count the change, he'd tell us how much we saved. At $4 per kid, he said, we didn't pay as much as the tickets they sold suckers on the weekends.

That all-day ticket was low-tech, just a string wrapped around my wrist and pinched together with a metal clamp colored distinctly for the day of the week. The picnic area was next to the German Beer Garden, just a few steps away from that ticket booth. The picnicking splash of concrete rested under picnic tables heavier and longer than ours at home. The sanded wood tops were painted green and orange, resting on the kind of metal legs I knew from school playgrounds.

On a trip when I would've been Nicky's age, Tina was too small to ride anything except the Western Cruise paddleboat, the Cedar Point & Lake Erie Railroad—complete with a conductor who shot bandits from the locomotive cab—or she could ride in my Dad's arms on Cedar Downs. The Downs were a racing ride with mechanical horses moving pell-mell like some manic carousel. Safety on the Downs was in the minds of the parents in that era. Those horses were flying at 25 miles an hour with little more than a leather belt over the kids riding, some of them even younger than Nicky.

After Dad would stow our cooler, me and my brother, both old enough to ride anything, were told to go have fun and meet back at the Fascination game center, the park's only air-conditioned building and a spot where Dad lingered to escape the heat. We lined up for the Blue Streak wooden coaster, loud and rude while it slammed us around its corners. In those days before full-body restraints on rides, a simple metal bar held us in place, a bar we needed to grip to keep from getting lifted out of the seats. But we threw up our arms at the top of the biggest hill and tossed caution into the Lake Erie winds. To hurry to the other end of the park, we'd take the sky ride, its four-seat cars swinging on a cable while lake breezes ran over our butch haircuts.

More than twenty-five years after that trip, we met Bob and Tina and her girls in the parking lot with hugs and shrieks. Nicky helped me tote the cooler into the picnic area. Hi-C Juice boxes replaced the can of Hawaiian Punch and plastic pitcher of Kool-Aid that I drank as a boy, but the PB&J was a constant between generations. The bread had darkened from lily-white Wonder loaves to healthier whole-wheat slices. The oversized bags of the Cain's potato chips of the Sixties became snack bags of Goldfish and Cheetos.

"What's next, kids?" I asked my nieces, girls I haven't seen in more than four years.

"Raptor!"

"Again?" Little Chelsea had been measured at the park office to verify that she was big enough to ride, and so she carried a special pass to show off at the entrance to the coasters. But she wasn't the most daring of riders.

"Mean Streak." Nicky stuffed his plastic sandwich bag inside his Cheetos bag, then tossed the wad into a trashcan.

A chorus of girl's voices answered, "Let's go."

My sister and brother and I looked at each other and remembered waiting for our lunches to settle before Mom would let us ride. "Well, you can ride it right now," I told the throng, "so long as we take the Sky Ride, and then the train out to Frontier Land."

Nicky rolled his eyes. "Okay, at least the Sky Ride anyway." From there kids would careen down the streets to the monster coaster. People could lose their lunches on the biggest rides, but it was a risk at fun I felt I ought to take. If my dad could avoid being the fun police—a task he usually left to my mom on those Cedar Point days—I could follow his example. I was in a place where even a rookie dad could splash out a hit.

IN MY SUMMER OF 1968, THE PARK'S MILL RACE RIDE was new enough to command lines as long as the blocks in our neighborhood. Dad was waiting with us while Mom tended to Tina, and he left his fancy stereo camera in her care as well. A jaunty, straw short-brim trilby hat kept the July sun off his forehead. I shuffled alongside him and drifted a few paces ahead of our spot.

"Keep your place in line," he told me. "Don't want them throwing you out."

"Dad."

"They would, you know."

"Okay. How much longer?"

"Long enough, for sure. You boys ready to get wet?"

July's heat made us certain we were eager. The Mill Race was unlike anything up to that year in the park's history, a ride that gave onlookers a thrill too. Riders floated in cars shaped like logs, bobbing on the lake water pumped in to carry the thrills. At the bottom of the steepest hill, the cars splashed water out of a massive sluice and onto anybody standing nearby. We rode up that hill in seats behind one another, Dad holding onto his hat in his lap, his glasses in his hand. The bareheaded man without his spectacles didn't look much like my dad, except for those moments when he'd nap on the couch.

The look on his face on that ride was not as tranquil, though. He rode next to Bob in the seat in front. "Hold on to that bar," he barked over his shoulder.

"I will, I will."

He muttered low enough to camouflage his commands. "No crap now. Behave." His not-on-my-watch worry floated in the air.

"This is fun!" Bob said at that moment. I saw dad's shoulders relax a little.

"Fun," I said, pumping up his idea.

The cars vibrated up a rubber belt to the top of a hill, then soared down on the water attached to nothing but our expectations. We hit the water and felt it cascade around us, dripping and sloshing into the car and around our Keds. Dad was lifting up his loafers.

"Wow, crap!" He turned around to look at me, water dripping off his face, his always-slicked-back hair now ignoring its Vitalis cream. "You're okay. We're all okay." He held up his hat as we skidded around a few more sluices of the ride.

OUT IN THE SLUICES OF 1994, NICKY AND I were bumping along after the biggest hill, amped up with log-cars now running side by side in the ride's 26th year of fun. We stepped off damp but not soaked, me wearing my Reds jersey in its resilient wool and Nicky with a Cubs tee that hung halfway to his knees.

"Enough?" I asked.

"I guess," he said. "I mean, there's more."

"More water. Of course."

"There's standing beside the bottom of that hill," my sister said. "I told him about it. You do wanna go there, don't you?"

At that point we'd walked miles to cover the entire park, from the gate-side picnic lockers to the waterborne rides of Frontier Town's lakeside. I looked at her and flashed on her seven-year-old ponytail during that year when the Mill Race was new. The bottom of that Mill Race hill still spilled water on everyone, riding or watching, just as it had 26 years earlier.

"To beside that hill we go," I said, leading us to the splash zone. When the cars hit the bottom, the lake water cascaded like it was poured from a bucket in the star-lined sky. I looked up and wiped my face and grinned for the camera that I'd handed off to a cousin. Dad never would've given up a camera in that moment, I thought as we mugged for the shot. But he knew

how to take us to a place where having fun was the work to be done. We walked the miles back to the lockers and then our car, dripping and grateful to be successful in our day's work, wet enough to hear the happiness squeaking in each sneakered step.

We drove toward the town of my boyhood. With each mile we slouched a little more in soggy seats with our five-day underwear. We were road trip men whose clothes hadn't seen a washer since last week.

"I'm feeling a little rashy," Nicky said. There were limits to how much walking we should've done while wet. The Cedar Point parking lot had been vast.

"We'll be at Tina's house pretty soon. She's got a washer."

"Even a dryer, too?"

I was so eager to keep his affection I didn't even hear the sarcasm. "Yes, a dryer. What was your favorite today?"

"Easy enough. The Magnum."

"And the second favorite?"

"The Magnum for the first time with you."

It was a tilt-a-whirl moment, maybe one he gave me because he knew how much I craved it. Nevertheless, it felt earned after the distance from Texas to the Lake Erie shoreline, the 1,648 miles reported by the Sunbird's odometer. My dad only had a 60-minute drive to Cedar Point. I congratulated myself on my extra fortitude, but Dad might have put as much emotional effort into his trip as I had with mine. Nicky and I tooled along Ohio Route 2, a local road that runs beside Erie's shallowest water.

There was no ballgame on that Cedar Point night for us to revel in. No recounting leaping catches, powerful drives, or a frozen lemonade that lasted for three whole innings because it was sold to us rock-hard. We let the miles of Route 2 wash past us like they always did on a return to Toledo from Cedar Point. McDonald's wrappers and bags were wadded up in the passenger well of the Sunbird after our drive-thru supper, the cheesy meat and fries doing their work to lull us both into early sleep. I blinked myself awake and dialed in the Tigers game. I didn't need to wonder where it was on the radio. The lakeshore was well within range of Detroit's powerful WJR. Ernie Harwell's Georgia drawl rolled off the speakers as the Tigers tried to score on the White Sox in Chicago.

The radio's glow lit the car just enough to illuminate Nicky dozing. It was the ninth at last for Detroit. A young David Wells was throwing for the Tigers against Sam McDowell, and Ernie told us the two pitchers had already combined for 15 strikeouts. Nobody was coming out of any bullpen to finish that game. Complete games were less rare in my childhood, so the lack of relievers on the night in 1994 grabbed my attention.

"Tettleton is ready at the plate, the last chance for the Tigers," Harwell said. "Full count. Nobody on." The sound of the White Sox crowd rose up like a kind of surf, breaking over the car. "And it's strike three, looking. He stood there like a house by the side of the road and watched it go by."

It was a signature Ernie strikeout call, rarely used for a Tigers batter, but Nicky wasn't awake to hear it. I nudged him with a line of my own. "Cedar Point will do that to you." No reply from his side. "Wear you out. In a good way."

"Magnum was the best," he mumbled in a voice dredged from sleep. He sat up a little and glanced at the shoreline. He dropped into the voices of Simpsons kids, squawking, "Are we there yet? Are we there yet? Are we there yet?"

Even though we were still 45 minutes away, I told him we were. In a way, I'd been in Toledo ever since we crossed out of the gates at Cedar Point. This time I was returning as a fresh player, up from the Texas League. Big leaguers do rehab stints down in the minors. Maybe this trip across the country was an emotional rehab. I believed there were no pitches in Toledo I hadn't already faced.

MINOR KEY MEMORY
Tides vs. Mud Hens
Ned Skelton Field, Toledo
Thursday, July 21

We'd been crossing the country with the resolve of Depression hoboes, always moving on to find the next best place. Thursday is often a travel day in the majors, so we scheduled a minor-league game in Toledo. I wanted my brother and sister to see what a successful dad I was compared to the failures of our father. I was ignoring my own failure of divorce.

There was no recrimination about that breakup as Nicky and I drove the streets of my blue-collar town, though. The story of my father's suicide still wasn't shared with him, much less explained. It was enough to reunite my boy with his cousins, the six nieces growing up in the town where every member of my family was born and raised. The girls were between 6 and 10 years old. They could share things with Nicky like basketball on a driveway in front of a garage and ice cream at the Dairy Queen, things I first shared with my brother. Like me, Bob had already passed through divorce by that summer. His second act of marriage was a sweet return, his fortune as profound as mine in finding a new partner. Bob was adding to his family. He'd fathered a son of his own in the springtime, a Seybold boy whose prospects for happiness were major-league.

Bob would lead the way on a trip to Toledo's minor-league park, a night with the Mud Hens in a county stadium that didn't try to pretend to the grandeur of The Jake or echoes of championships at Riverfront. Ned Skelton Field was the best ballpark Toledo could offer, and I loved Bob for ensuring that our string of ballgames was restarting right after our Cedar Point respite.

I was mistaken on that Thursday about what the whole trip represented, though. I believed by the seventh day of our vacation I was showing Nicky the best of what a game and a family trip could deliver. I might have known, however, that a swing by Point Place, the only neighborhood where I ever played as a boy, would bring back memories better left undisturbed. I took Nicky on a tour of the old neighborhood alone. I navigated the Sunbird down streets so narrow they felt like a pair of childhood pants that didn't fit anymore.

"They're all named after numbers," he said in his seat beside me, eyeing the street markers in the neighborhood that was still as white as any loaf of Wonder Bread.

"Not all of them, but pretty much. There's Edgewater Drive, and Summit Street."

"Places you played?" He popped in another stick of Big League Bubble and looked over one street after another, covered in Fifties tract houses, their single-story aluminum siding in a peacock of colors, punctuated by the high toned red brick we associated with families better than our average.

"Not really," I said. "We played on the streets where our houses sat, a few blocks over, maybe."

"And here, I guess," he said while we passed the city pool that was built over the edge of the Detwiler swamp.

"Before the pool at the water plant, and after too."

"Water at a plant?"

I spun the Sunbird's wheel and started us down Suder Avenue. "Water treatment plant. They made fertilizer here."

"Out of shitty water."

"That's important to the process," I said. "You need something nasty to grow something better. There were bags of it, that fertilizer, all laid out in a tiny warehouse a few blocks away from our house."

The radio was playing WTTO's Top 40 while we cruised, a string of mysterious songs that were current but peppered with hits I knew from my decades in the town. The screams of Jimmy Page's Led Zeppelin guitar lulled us both into a mirror of quiet. But while Green Day started up with "Welcome to Paradise," Nicky probed further.

"You just played, out on the streets?"

"Everybody did. They didn't really care where, so long as we weren't in trouble. Come home when the street lights come on."

"That's cool."

"Hard to say how cool, but it felt normal. You found kids you liked on your block, or maybe in your school. Hung out together."

"Let's put the top down," he said to me, holding an arm out the window to let the muggy Maumee Bay air run over his hands.

"Let's," I said as I pulled in front of a house with the aluminum awnings that most of those addresses wore, striped like billiard balls and propped up by black metal posts that flanked the front porches. I peeled down our rag-top and opened the talk about my boyhood, the days when I'd leave the house with my brother to make a summer day.

"You walked, I guess."

"Rode bikes, more often. Big banana seat on a gold Sting Ray."

"What happened to that?" He asked a question I hadn't considered in more than twenty years.

"Gave that bike away, I guess. My mom did. After I left. But that bike took me everywhere by the time I was getting to be your age."

We sat and just watched the afternoon foot traffic on 289th street. I turned down the FM radio and then reached toward my past and put the AM on. At 800 on the dial, CKLW up in Windsor still belted out hippie rock and rhythm and blues. They were in a middle of a set that included the Stones' "Satisfaction." I was transported to that year with that bike and no supervision to speak of.

Those were days of rebellion for many kids, but I was only on the cusp of my grand battles with Dad. I hadn't yet gotten comfortable with arguing with him, not even when he'd sail off into racist slurs during that summer of 1968 about the riots that followed Martin Luther King's assassination. They were niggers and shiftless and lazy, he said, talk that was my first taste of venom not directed at us, or some wayward nail on a workbench Dad didn't pound straight. He didn't care if we agreed with him out loud. But dissent seemed forbidden. His rants gave me a place to take my early steps, though.

"Damn police. Why don't they do their job? Bastards," he said to us during dinner after looting broke out south of Dorr Street. Blacks lived there in a city little more desegregated than any other in the white-bread Midwest.

"They're supposed to shoot 'em?" I wondered what the rules were, and if they were anything like the TV war dramas like *Combat*.

"Damn right. They're taking over."

"But I don't see them here."

"They damn well better not come up here. I'll shoot 'em myself."

Just downstairs in the basement, a handsome set of rifle, billy club, and sawed off shotgun hung on the wall of his workshop. Dad seemed capable of anything he'd crow about. The pork chops were salted and cut and chewed while the kitchen table grew quiet.

"Did you see any when you grew up?"

He looked up and pointed his knife. "Enough, for sure. We'd run 'em off the street when they'd hang around Galena Street."

"You used a gun?"

"No, not needed. A pop bottle. Cracked one guy's head wide open."

That story, again. "But why? Were they rioting? I don't get it."

"They were niggers in our neighborhood. They didn't belong."

"Because they didn't live there?"

He slammed down his fork. "You don't want to ask more questions about all that. They deserved what they got. They stole." He was glaring, then turned his gaze back to his plate. "The cops didn't do their jobs then, either."

I poked the bear. "So you were in a gang, then?"

"Goddammit, Ronny. You sound like you love 'em. Do you? Huh?"

"I just don't… I wanna know what they ever did to you. That's all."

"Niggers don't deserve an explanation. Stop asking questions." Dad hurled out the last sentence like the crack of the bullwhip that he hung off a nail in his workshop.

"Eat your peas, Ronny," my mom said. "Too much talking, not enough eating." I watched my dad's face soften at her words, and then he lifted a glare at her.

"I see what you're doing," he told her.

"Let's just eat," she said, her voice rising.

"You lived with 'em, too. You know."

"I went to school with them. Coloreds aren't all bad."

"Let's see them take care of a family like I do." He sawed into the pork chop. With that, it was settled. He made our rules in our tract house: the louder you were, the more right you must be.

In the Sunbird, Nicky looked at the adults and a few kids on the street. "You know any of these people anymore?"

"It's been about 20 years since I lived here."

"We could take a walk."

"We should, yes. I gotta warn you, though. Evergreen Terrace this ain't."

"Not like the Simpsons."

"Well," I said as I opened the car door, "we had neighbors we didn't like, just like Homer and Ned Flanders."

"But they're not here now."

"I don't know, really. Let's have a look at my house here."

We stopped on the sidewalk in front of 4528, its windows still bearing the two blue service stars from the years when Bob and I were both in the Army. I looked into the picture window across the front and saw my reflection, even from the edge of a yard that couldn't be more than 20 feet deep. Small yards. I saw the pane of the window where I'd put up a handwritten note for my neighborhood pals. *I have tonsillitis*, it said, explaining why I couldn't come out and play.

"We ran all up and down this street," I said, reaching for a memory more sweet. "Kickball like baseball. With the sewer grates and trees for bases."

"The cars didn't run you over?"

"We'd yell, 'Car!'"

"No real baseball, huh?"

I eyed the edge of the front lawn, hard up against the two-ribboned driveway, the boundary for the game of 50-Cent where I learned to be a base runner. I ran between those driveways but didn't escape the place until years later.

"Dad taught me to throw straight and fast in that game. We'd try to slide under a throw."

"And bats. You had bats."

"Just plastic. All those windows," I said, pointing at the storm doors on the fronts of houses.

"Like something out of, I dunno, like *The Cosby Show*."

"Well, not much like that. Nobody black ever lived here." I walked a bit farther down the sidewalk. "See that? My old room." I pointed at the attic window, next to the TV antenna tower still standing beside the house.

"No blacks. Kinda racist, huh?"

I heard a voice that wanted to argue, like my own when I lived in that bedroom. "I guess you're right. Not much integration here in Point Place. Nothing to integrate."

"But you liked baseball then, right?"

"More every year, as I got older."

"Because, there's lots of blacks in baseball," he said, cracking his gum. "Even then."

"What's with all of this?"

"I'm just saying." He stopped a few steps away from me.

"Yes, you are saying." I closed my eyes. "And I'm listening. You're right. My people were racists." The family legend was that Dad voted for George Wallace in '68. Said he always canceled out mom's liberal vote. He must have loved that control over her.

We stood in front of the house where I learned to argue with Dad and looked at the attic window. A man walked up his driveway. "Can I help you?"

"Just looking," I said.

Nicky chimed in. "It's the house where he grew up."

"You're from here, then."

"We're Seybolds. My dad helped build that house. Parts of it, anyway. The garage. That attic bedroom."

"Okay," said the fellow, lifting a little smile. "I just wanted to know why you were stopped here."

"It's a public street. He's my boy. We're just visiting."

"Hey, it's okay. I got a right to ask, right?"

"Sure you do," I said evenly. Nicky was watching me closer than the fellow who stood in his driveway. "I mean, hey, we're all from here. You ever take your kids to where you were born?"

"You bet. Out in Maumee. We moved in here 10 years ago."

He mentioned the suburb where we were headed for the night's ballgame, so I tried to make a little nice with him. "We're going to see the Mud Hens tonight."

"With the boy. Where're you coming from?"

"A long way from here," I said, looking at my son and feeling the miles again.

"Texas," Nicky added. "Austin, Texas." His voice hinted that the town was his genuine home, even as we stood in front of mine. My home field became Austin after I'd left what I considered a minor-league town.

Dad's death cemented my exit from Toledo. What good would telling Nicky Dad's dark tale do for the homey memory we were enjoying? I didn't know how to say it, wondered if it was the right time, and then recoiled from the challenge. It was a spot of shame, like the oil stain I could see in the driveway that Dad had once kept so pristine.

Instead of revealing the secret of Dad's death, I told Nicky about playing on that driveway. Chain-link fence ran along both sides of it. The concrete was already brushed smooth by the time I began to play on it, bouncing a basketball. The garage door was only one car wide but had two windows, each bigger than an ironing board. The door was pulled down low on the basketball evenings, but not completely. Protect those garage windows. Mom backed the station wagon off the drive and parked it beside the screen door at the side of the house.

The chain link tops, twisted into points on the fence next to Mrs. Suzer's house, would dig into my back whenever I dove to rebound the ball. The backboard, regulation size and forever white, hung like a badge in the front peak of the lime green garage. Atop the peak, a single outdoor floodlight taunted us, waiting to be broken with a too-high shot. The shot never occurred, another unrealized anxiety of Dad's. In time, he created safety bars around the light.

Nicky and I drove back to my sister's house, taking one turn onto Ottawa River Road, another onto Suder, past the fruit stands and finally onto Tina's Michigan country road, Sterns. Part of our route matched the one I used to take on my Sting Ray bike. But on the road to Tina's house, while Nicky busied himself with his Game Boy, I allowed myself to add up what brought me back home. I felt the ache of old despair creeping in, driving with my boy in the middle of a trip to prove that I knew more about loving than my Dad. He did his best at love, but he threw wild. Love gave him a no-decision when he'd pitched.

"Whatcha thinking, Dad?" Not a question I could ask my father, but Nicky was asking.

"About my dad," I said. I glanced at him as I turned onto Tina's street. Dad had been gone more than fifteen years, time that had repaired some parts of me. "Sometimes I miss him."

"He died, right?"

"Passed away. When I was not a teenager anymore."

"So you were twenty?" He tugged on his cap as I sped up the car.

"Almost twenty-one. He never got to meet you. He would've loved you."

It was quiet as we pulled up to my sister's house. Before Nicky climbed out, before his cousins greeted him at the door, before we came back into a house of love my sister built, he said, "I'd miss you, too." It was enough to chase away my ache over Dad.

LATER THAT NIGHT WE WERE SLUMMING IN THE MINORS between big league stops. The Mud Hens were playing in a stadium with a thicket of bleacher seats. Bob reserved us genuine seats with backs. There was enough family to require two different rows to sit near each other. Unlike the major league games, the minors' players were mysterious, the men sometimes struggling with efforts that gave us comedy to accompany their plays.

In Toledo the locals called the sodas pop, white and red striped boxes carried the popcorn, and the program had stapled pages instead of glued-in sheets. But we took down the batting orders and names and positions as if they were legends, entering the players on the Bibb Falk like they were witnesses to our game, instead of we to theirs.

The slack time of every ball game wrapped itself around the whole Seybold family, those born and those tied in by marriage. Between the trips to the cotton candy stand, aside from the moments when we logged the dimly-lit plays between the Hens and Norfolk Tides, I reached back to the moment on the sidewalk.

"He was just checking us out," I told Nicky.

"The popcorn guy?"

"No, the guy this afternoon."

"Yeah," he said, writing another 4-3 into a box on the program's score sheet. Ground ball to second. "I think he was worried we were burglars or something."

"Or gang members."

"Like in *My Cousin Vinny*," Nicky said.

"Yeah. Youths."

"Yutes?" He did his best Fred Gwynne imitation. "Yutes?"

My brother overheard this. "You gotta watch those yutes."

We were laughing and reaching for popcorn when the crack of a bat made everybody's head turn. High up, into the minor-league lights that can still leave bits of the outfield in shadow, a baseball sailed. Out toward the chain-link fence that marked a home run, where the right fielder just looked at it flying over his head.

"At least it didn't break a window," Nicky said.

"Nothing worse than that," I replied.

"Something you could expect from yutes," my sister added.

I grabbed a handful of cotton candy off a niece's cone.

"Hey Uncle Ron, you didn't ask."

I handed it to Nicky. "What are you complaining about? I didn't take it."

Nicky started to nibble. "It's okay," he said, then pointed to me. "Just ask him for more."

I reached into my wallet for another five-dollar bill, ready to hand it to a niece.

"Your money's no good here," my brother said. "I got tonight."

"No good tomorrow night, either," my sister added. "You guys spent money to get here."

I felt a little bump in my heartbeat, like a skip of a rock over Maumee Bay. "You guys."

My niece looked at me, then at Nicky. "Getting here. That was the hard part, I bet."

"Yeah, well, not so hard," he said. "We're Flying Rabbits, you know. Road guys."

We stayed for the whole game, right down to the last batter the Mud Hens sent to the plate in a loss. Our victory was off the field, because it was the very last time all three families of kids sat at a game together. We drove the sleeping kids home across the Anthony Wayne Bridge and back to the northern suburbs. The youngest ones we toted into the house while Nicky and his oldest cousin held open the screen door. We were a team, my family, a unit bred in a minor league town. I wanted to believe we'd grown into adults with better home bases than our parents gave us.

GAME 6

STORM WARNING
Royals vs. Tigers
Tiger Stadium, Detroit
Friday, July 22

While the sun rose in the Michigan sky the next day, a mower blared outside my sister's window. The smell of fresh cut grass wafted through the screen, a scent that carried me to summer mornings when I was Nicky's age. The engine cut off and then started up, then cut off again. I lay abed and listened to the silences surrounding that mower.

Silence often hung in the air after Dad's defeatist diagnoses. As the son of a doctor he always knew more than anyone about what was wrong with him—bursitis, diverticulitis, gallstones, and his apprehensions about everything even worse. He'd pronounce a sentence on himself that was met by stunned silence. We dared not disagree.

Then there was the silence that is immeasurable in meaning. Summer storms beside Lake Erie produced a silence, the absence of the sound of wind after an hour of gusts so hard they'd whistle through the narrow windows atop our basement walls. That silence cemented a fear of weather that lasted into my fatherhood. Dad could be as sudden as that weather.

He grew up in the silent spaces behind his older brother's sass. Dad told stories about the battles between his brother NJ and his father. In one story, his father pulled a prank whose punch line was serving NJ a dinner of dog shit under a covered serving tray. Dad would tell the tale and uncork a cackle, a hard sound deeper than the usual guffaws brothers enjoy when a sibling gets in trouble.

In my sister's house I wriggled my toes in bed, reveling in the kind of silence of a day whose game was just one hour up the road. That silence was a messenger of happiness, quiet time that carried me back to boyhood summer vacations when the box fan in our window stopped cooling our attic bedroom. Once the Great Lakes weather got too hot for any fan, I'd get up and pour a bowl of Trix and splash on whole milk. I touched my scalp in my sister's house to feel for the buzz cut I wore in that boyhood summer, as if my hair were cropped that close.

The scent of the grass mingled with the smell of bacon in the kitchen. I roused Nicky and padded down the hall to the kitchen, where he hoovered up the crispy strips along with Frosted Flakes. Our mornings up to then had been filled with Egg McMuffins or snatched danishes or donuts from hotel lobbies. That day's tickets would admit us to Tiger Stadium, home of the only championship that stirred my dad's heart.

At our quiet breakfast table I searched for a memory of any major league game with my dad. It might've been Tiger Stadium, because it was a park within a same-day drive. For Dad, a casual fan of baseball with driving anxieties, it could as well as have been a week's drive away. He'd grouse about battling the traffic on I-75 as if it were a swim against the Niagara River.

A game printed on the back of the cereal box helped me drift into the only nine innings I could recall with Dad. It would have been leaner than any nine innings with Nicky. That game with Dad was in the summer of 1973. Long stretches of silence played out between us then, moments awash in sounds of the rhythms of baseball. They would widen the gulf. By the afternoon of that game, Dad had abdicated his throne of tough-guy swagger. He was just starting a slide into the ferocious depression that pulled him down like an undertow on a beach.

He might've sat a little too close to me on that day in Tiger Stadium. The ballpark would be crowded. Dad would be showing off like I learned to, a lover of the showy flourish instead of everyday parenting magic. He drove to the ballpark at Woodward and Trumbull streets on a weekend afternoon to hunt down a spot after he complained about plowing through the traffic and the crowds. It was a day in July, but I'd be wearing bell-bottom jeans and a pair of Converse All-Stars. Dad would wear his Bermuda shorts.

I hadn't sat beside him for anything longer than a Cedar Point coaster ride or a spin on a Ferris wheel there. At my breakfast table with Nicky, I closed in on the game-day details with Dad that I wanted to be true. He'd returned home early and alone from a family California vacation. I'd stayed away from that trip like a teenager does while asserting independence. By taking me to Tiger Stadium before the rest of the family returned, Dad was showing off with an outing to prove he was a fun father.

He bought a program but would not mark the scorecard inside it. He flipped through its pages like he was turning the pale orange pages of the *Toledo Blade* Peach Section listings, looking for a TV show.

"Indians are up first," he said.

"I know, Dad."

"So what else do you know?"

"Leflore bats third."

He handed me the program. "Horton at cleanup." Then he rattled off the rest of the Tigers batting order. Many heroes of that championship team five years earlier were still with the team in 1973. Free agency was brand new. Players didn't migrate on their own.

"Hey, Dad, pretty good. Even I don't know the Tigers that well."

"You're a Reds fan. How would you know?"

"Well, the Tigers are okay, too."

"Champs. Not like your Reds." Cincinnati had fallen short the season before, losing the Series in seven games in a heartbreaker.

I'd watch the passions run across his face as I often did when he challenged me, the evil I would search out in his looks while we fought with words and worse. I looked out on the field as Bill Freehan, one of the heroes of that championship 1968 Tiger team, crouched behind the plate. The first few innings would draw nothing good from Dad but his shouts when two Indians struck out to wrap up an inning. He'd grouse about the Tiger pitcher Mickey Lolich—another Series hero and still wearing a gut like Dad once did—coughing up homers.

There was a kind of quiet between us that I mistook for peace. There were no marks of age on his face, his chin bearing that tight-trimmed goatee that he sprouted as I turned into a combative teenager. That peace I imagined coming off Dad was different than his belly laughs at Shecky Green's standup on the Dean Martin summer show. That absence of rage, the moments of his silence and long sighs, were marks of losses to come.

"Now how about a double play?" he said without enough volume to call it a shout.

The Indians hitter rapped the ball into the infield. "There it goes," I said, looking over at him.

"Just like I said, huh?" A small grin crept up from his goatee. Maybe that expression was what Dad's peace looked like. We were trying to play together on that ballpark afternoon with all of its kinds of quiet.

I blinked and promised myself at the breakfast table that my morning was holding a different kind of quiet. I looked up to see Nicky munching. He made his own effort to reach into my past. "Dad, did you go to games as a kid?"

"Hardly any, really."

"Not even to play?"

"I didn't when I was your age. Couldn't afford it." He looked at me, puzzled. "My brother Bob and I, we had gloves and a bat, but no encouragement to join teams. We asked."

"They wouldn't let you?"

"We had to tell our parents there'd be a fee to join Little League. Then Mom told us about how Dad never got to play in any league as a kid."

This was news in Nicky's world. All of it was new, because just as it was for Dad, there were few stories I shared about my father. He remained a secret in his imperfections.

"So what did the money have do with it?"

"Mom said we were poor." Nicky munched as I mulled over the poverty Dad claimed whenever it provided a reason to say no about spending. Being poor was the chorus of a song with verses that Dad didn't learn in his own childhood. Mom knew firsthand about living on relief, as she called welfare, staying in a rent house with three brothers and only two bedrooms. Dad's tales about being poor were always a chorus of how little everyone had during those years. He had no verses of his own to sing about hard times. If Dad told a story of 1938, it would have been about a lakeside cottage and a father with staff privileges at the biggest Catholic hospital in Toledo.

"So no baseball for ya," Nicky said. "Basketball?"

"There was no basketball after baseball season ended, either. Not in our Catholic school without a gym. Instead of sports we played in basements in the winters. Like the one you played in when we came up here years ago."

"Tina's basement."

"Actually Bob's. And we had one like that, but bigger." Some parts were finished out and another had washer-dryer-ironing board, plus a laundry sink that gave off a relentless odor of Clorox. We never called it bleach. I grew up in a name-brand family.

I wanted to show Bob and Tina how I'd grown up to be someone more than my dad. He would've told me to add it all up, though. Dad didn't buy any baseball tickets on credit like I did. He lived a cash life. Paying for tickets to see his team lose would be more rotten luck. I was taking my son to games like a dad who could afford to watch a loss. I got up from the table and dressed in my freshly laundered Reds jersey, the costume of a guy who didn't flinch at cost—not even when I'd add it up beforehand and then afterward with regret.

As my Frosted Flakes grew soggy in the bowl of milk, I hovered toward a sweeter memory. Tiger Stadium hosted the only sports joy I ever shared with Dad, a breakthrough season when I was Nicky's age and first touched the power of rooting for a home team together.

DAD WAS A MAKER WHEN MAKING AND FIXING WAS EXPECTED of a man, rather than celebrated. His glories included a stereo console he built and packed with hand-wired components; the half-walls he erected to carve up our basement into faux rooms, each with knotty pine paneling and plastic windows colored by stained-glass atop them; or a rotisserie motor he rigged with a timer to twist chickens over the grill on a schedule. While the birds cooked over the coals, Dad would turn on the Tigers game. We were told every inning the broadcast was brought to us by Stroh's Beer. The sound of baseball during that year melded with the growl of that rotisserie as the cheap broiler chickens rotated.

The Tigers played far better in 1968 than any of their seasons since I was born. "Extraordinary," Dad would say, one of the words he would teach me by accident. He taught me about strikeouts, either swinging or a strike three, looking—Ernie Harwell's call over that radio on any called strike three would be, "He stood there like a house at the side of the road." But then there were sacrifice flies, plays Dad never explained. If that fly ball was an out, it didn't matter to me.

Some of Dad's baseball lessons came up like the dandelions in our yard, natural and unplanted. If I'd ask him questions about baseball or the soldiers on TV, the Tigers hitting of long bombs versus bombing the Viet Cong. He would supply answers. But we'd stumble with the language between us. I spoke the slang of a pre-teen.

"So Dad, why do the Cardinals suck, anyway?"

He laughed a little too hard that day. "Do they, huh? Are you sure? They won the Series last year."

"They're not as cool as the Tigers. Kaline, McLain, wow."

"Cardinals had better pitching last year, kiddo. Better off the mound, we say."

But I wanted to scrap. Our family argued like bluegills sucking on Ottawa River lagoon scum. "Pitching, huh. So what if Gibson's got the best earned run percentage?"

"It's Earned Run Average. And you know he does. Won last year's Series for 'em, too."

"So? I mean, how come they won't win—"

He cut me off. "Not enough guys on that team named Gibson. Not this year. Gotta have a rotation, Ronny."

I watched the chickens turn over the coals. "So what's that then? Rotation." I crouched down a ways off the grill, right at his feet and looking up. I knew he liked that.

"In a rotation, they pitch one guy after another." He looked down at me. "You've got your mighty Denny McLain, see. Then Lolich. Then maybe a day off, then Schumaker. But after a few Series games, you can't be sure who's gonna pitch. You get it, right?"

I said that I did, unsure if it was true. What I took away from his lesson was not everything could be trusted to stay the same. You had to expect the worst to happen every time, even if everything had been perfect just up to that moment.

Those 1968 Tigers had the flashiest pitcher in the game heading into the Series. Denny McLain was an avid gambler, played the Hammond organ in a Detroit nightclub on nights when he didn't pitch, and won almost every game he started that season. He threw 28 complete games. Baseball was a blue-collar job. A starter was expected to throw every fourth day, 20 percent more than a 1994 starter's workload. Great pitchers, I was taught, finished what they started.

McLain was supposed to be invincible in the Series. My Dad said so, although baseball was a new place for him to trumpet his expertise. Dad was louder than usual in predicting McLain, a pitcher who'd make history with both MVP and Cy Young awards, would make the difference.

"Starters like him come along once in a lifetime," Dad said over the peas at our table set for five with captain's chairs at every place.

"We know, daddy," my mom said from the safety behind the kitchen's bar. She called him the same name we used, stirring her spaghetti sauce considered authentic because she'd lace it with oregano. It was a spice we tasted on no other supper night.

"Don't tell me he's not the best," he said. "Won thirty-one games."

"That's a record?" I asked.

"Not exactly. What does that matter? They yanked him out of that last game of the season too quick when he was ahead. He coulda tied the record."

"Why'd they do that?"

"Rest. That's what that old manager said. Wanted to rest him for the Series. Bastards."

I took a sip of milk. "You don't like the Tigers then?"

"Hell no. I mean yes, I like 'em. They're my team. Our team, anybody who has any sense."

"Then who's the bastards?"

"Ronny, listen. It's anybody who screws you over when you've earned something." I looked down at the plastic melamine plate where my spaghetti noodles waited for mom's ground beef sauce. "Like those bastards down at the station." Channel 13 where he worked was always The Station, like some railroad depot on a line to desolation. "You don't get it, but you will. Baseball, that's easy to understand. And pitching, that's everything."

"What about the hitting?" my brother asked.

"Hah. Who's doing any hitting this year? Tell me."

That was the season when the pitchers were kings and batting averages at all time lows. Gibson had a starter's season ERA of 1.12. I didn't know baseball before Dad started to love it out loud that year. He was a bandwagon fan, but once that kind of wagon starts rolling, nobody wants to argue about who is fan enough.

During that season's afternoons while Harwell's voice played out over those speakers, Dad reached back in his soul like a pitcher winding up. Dad was raising sons, taking the ball to do something as well as his father. Over that grill in our driveway and out from the redoubt of his basement, Dad could embrace the role of nurturer, however briefly.

Things soon looked dark for Tiger fans like Dad during that year's Series. Rain clouds roared up around Tiger Stadium during the fourth game. The rain delay meant McLain couldn't come back to pitch once the skies cleared, because he'd stopped pitching during the delay. His arm cooled. Baseball became a cheat to Dad as the Tiger hero fell short of Dad's dreams. "They're done, dammit," he said when he switched off the TV on that stormy afternoon. "Damn rain."

The Tigers had tumbled down three games to one in the Series. Dad was certain bad things would be getting worse. A Tigers title emerged eventually, thanks to the portly Lolich's historic win in Game 7, his third complete game of the Series. Dad didn't sense any better outcome might be in the air of that Series, just like I didn't expect a change in the weather on the road to our Tigers game.

AFTER A MATINEE OF SCHWARZENEGGER'S TRUE LIES on our own Tigers Friday, we emerged from Toledo's Showcase Cinema to a band of thick indigo clouds north of the city. Yonder lay Detroit. We had enough time to get to the city before the first pitch, I believed, but only if we could scurry underneath those clouds.

"It'll be okay," I told Nicky. "It's just some rain. That convertible has a top, you know."

Every mile into Michigan unfurled a deeper dread. I twisted the knob on the radio to hunt down weather bulletins. WJR, no, WXYZ—what was the biggest radio station in Detroit anymore? I bounced across a station with a snippet of "small craft warnings for this afternoon and evening" and tried to find another forecast during the 6 PM broadcasts. Nothing. Then the drops started to spatter onto the hood and our roof.

When I heard the hail, I was already skiing on the puddled Interstate. It pounded down hard enough to limit the view ahead to less than the length of a car. Taillights winked on. Beside me, Nicky was as still as a foul pole.

This would be it. The bad news of a slick highway would turn into the worse of our accident. Safety first? Well, that was a lie, or we'd be back in Toledo waiting this out. We'd dodged our share of misfortune up to now, with that cruise through the ghetto of Kansas City and the dented hotel room door of Cincinnati. Here, in the end, a force of nature would take us down. But I kept driving, trying to believe that it would let up. The wipers on the Sunbird stuttered in futility. There we'd be, an item on Detroit's Channel 7 where "a Texas man and his son were victims of multi-car pileup." A more sensible man would pull over, but where? The shoulders were littered with cars and trucks waiting it out. Braking to pull over would be just another danger.

Around 8 Mile Drive, the light started to peek through heavy clouds. The road's puddles gave the convertible a chance to shoot waves of rainwater onto the shoulders, but at least the hail wasn't pounding on the roof anymore. We pulled into a razor-wired parking lot with the place to ourselves. There was a game tonight, right? The paralyzing weather wouldn't give us our first rainout, would it? The lot began to fill up with those cars that pulled over in the storm.

The ballpark gave off an air of history, including my images of TV games and a dim memory of that afternoon with Dad. Tiger Stadium was the last remaining ballpark with a double-decked grandstand all the way around the field. It was the second-oldest park in the majors and a throwback from 1915.

That night's game would be the first one played in Detroit since the All Star Break, so the team billed it as Opening Day II, complete with Laser Light Fireworks afterward. Nicky and I walked the ancient aisles while the navy blue tarp still covered the infield. The delay plus the drive back to Toledo would make it a late night for us. Saturday morning we'd be speeding across the turnpike to Chicago. Even with the clouds parting, the game might still be called off as a rainout, since so much water pounded the field. Outfield drainage was not a prime feature of a 79-year-old baseball shrine.

Weather was the wild card I could never plan for. All I had on my side was belief that Major League Baseball never wanted to cancel a game, because making it up meant finding an open date in an overcrowded schedule. Especially during that year. The threat of a player's strike was making every game a financial necessity.

Rumblings of a strike arrived just as my tickets began to appear in the mailbox. In that era before the Web, returning tickets for games cancelled due to a strike would be complicated. After the labor unrest reared up, I had to gamble on the trip I'd already planned out. I didn't like the threat of losing hundreds of dollars on our tickets, or being held hostage to the whims of millionaire ballplayers angling for more pay. While the strike stoked my anxiety about our string of games, a rainout in Detroit would be a complete loss, unless my brother or sister wanted to use the rain checks.

We never talked about the strike. Even mentioning it seemed like tempting fate. We talked a lot of baseball. Team fielding averages, extra-base hits in extra innings. Nicky and I lugged around the inch-thick Baseball Guide, and just for extra measure, Street and Smith's annual magazine. We had one talk about who was the biggest cheater on the mound, the pitcher most likely to doctor up the ball and how he'd do it.

As the groundskeepers rolled the tarp off the wet field, a rock band wailed from a shelter underneath the centerfield scoreboard. Rock in Detroit was still called music from the Motor City. My brother arrived along with his daughter Ashley and delivered a weather update.

"They had tornadoes break out," he announced. "Nobody was killed, but there were semis that rolled over."

"Wow," was all Nicky could manage. His tennis shoes still squeaked from the parking lot puddles we'd crossed.

"Tornadoes. We cheated death, I guess." Bob and I shared a look at the word tornado. I brushed away an image of the Palm Sunday night when a twister passed through our suburb. We still considered that Sunday night a brush with death. To get my son to Tiger Stadium in time for First Pitch, I didn't have the sense to stop driving into the teeth of a tornado.

Once Nicky and I had outrun the weather, the ballpark became a treasure recovered. The night was the first on our trip where t-shirts were slung into the stands, the Tiger Toss. I saw the outfield decks for the first time under the lights. Then a rainbow appeared over that grandstand roof, spanning a space from left field to right. Tiger Stadium was beaten down and waterlogged, but it delivered the only rainbow of any of our ballparks. A rudimentary Jumbotron glowed behind left field. "I'm gonna go get wet," Nicky said, weaving his way down the rail and into the last of the rains. Video on the board showed shots of earlier rain delays. The weather threatened to wash out Bleacher Beach Party Night, a promotion to lure fans to the Friday cheap seats. The Tigers ran a tight and aged ship. The most expensive seats were in the level I'd bought for the family at $15 each. A family-size bag of peanuts was $3.

I chirped into our tape recorder that there was a Jumbotron in every park on our trip.

"Except for Wrigley," Nicky said.

"We don't know that. We haven't been there yet."

"Well, they didn't last year. I was there." Indeed, he'd already been to Wrigley with his stepdad. Once again I pushed away the fact I'd be the second man to take him to that landmark.

He might have seen my face cloud. "But Little Caesar's is so easy to find here," he added, "because the guy who owns Little Caesar's also owns the Tigers."

Of that game I remember little, so bathed in relief I was at our safe arrival. Tiger outfielders saved home runs with catches at the wall in the middle innings. In one high moment, Tony Phillips took off on a dead run for the warning track the instant a fly ball left the bat. The catches rattled the home crowd's cheers around the pillars that obstructed some views. Old ballparks like Detroit's had bad seats, usually sold for less. Later the Tigers made a moment we'd mark in the Bibb Falk and circle like I did as a sportswriter. In the bottom of the eighth, with the Tigers trying to go ahead for good, Kirk Gibson came to the plate. A World Series hero from the '80s and the oldest man on the team, Gibson pounded a pitch into that deck in right field for a game-capping homer. The ball came down in the spot where that rainbow had ended.

Nicky and Bob and I jumped in the puddles in our row while the half-full stands erupted. "Gibby!" I said, invoking Gibson's nickname.

"A tater," Nicky said, clutching the rolled-up program under his arm to keep it off the wet seat.

"Long ball, so long," Bob said.

From a radio in the row behind us we heard Harwell's signature home run call. "That one is loooong gone," he crooned.

"Worth driving through a tornado for," I said.

"Our lucky night," Nicky said. He tapped me on the head with his program.

"Why, I oughta moyder you," I said, evoking the Stooges with the line and waving a clenched fist.

"Quiet, you," he replied. It was a night of the home team winning, the team Dad thought of as home.

WE RODE BACK BY THE GLOW OF STREETLIGHTS punctuated by oncoming high-beams. The headlights splayed our shadows across the car's headliner. Harwell's post-game wrap up was on the radio and it was just him and the two of us, as cocooned as foxes in a den. Was our time in the convertible a balm to repair scars from the day I had to leave Nicky's house for good? I didn't dare think how that day felt to a boy just turning six. Maybe Nicky asked for his bedtime story from his mom that evening, just to hear someone's voice who loved him. While he heard her words he felt the swoosh of his waterbed as he turned onto his side to listen. His eyelids fluttered and he gripped the soft flannel of the blanket with its firemen and police on it. Whatever he dreamt, no one would know. He may have kept the sadness locked inside, because the grown ups would fight if he said anything about it.

We still hadn't talked about what he might have pined for on that first night, with his mom making up for my absence. I had to ask him about it anyway, because I wanted to know if he'd cried. I needed his memory of that night so I could share my own memories of that house with him.

"Did it make you sad on the weekend when I left?"

"Which weekend?"

"That first one," I said, as I navigated us through a little maze of ramps to get us away from Detroit. "When it was still Hanukkah, and it wasn't Christmas yet."

"We didn't have a tree that year."

"Yeah. We didn't ever have trees for the holiday, did we?"

"But we always had lights. Blue and white. All on that window." He paused and looked away from me and out his window. "I liked the light and the way it was in my room that winter."

"Yeah, great lights." I congratulated myself. I sold his mom on the idea of Hanukkah being the Festival of Lights. I put up blue and white lights in his room. "You know, I had holiday lights in my house growing up."

"Hey, Dad." There was that music again, the hey dad. "Your dad didn't ever have to leave you to live somewhere else, did he?"

I felt a chill on my neck. No, Dad didn't leave us while I lived at the house. I would answer Nicky's question without details, omitting those facts I still believed he wasn't ready to hear—and I wasn't ready to tell.

"No, he didn't leave."

"He didn't have to, did he?" When I stayed quiet, he added, "You did, though—I guess."

"Guess so. But we're together now." I reached over to chuck him on the shoulder. "It's been fun, you know?" It was the missing moments of our life in Austin that made our trip fun. I brought him the breakfasts I was missing on all of his school mornings, then served him his suppers out of ballpark concession stands and off McDonald's counters. Beside me in the car he nodded off, leaning against the door, his window open to the damp summer air. I reached over and tapped his door lock button again, just to make sure he was safe with me.

DAY GAME DAD
Reds vs. Cubs
Wrigley Field
Saturday, July 23

Game days popped up on our calendar like the peach stands that littered summer roads back in the Texas Hill Country. Our stops were delicious moments, filled with promise we could smell as we got close, then taste in the moments of a game. So far we'd found our game times at a Texas sunset, on a Great Plains summer night, alongside the Ohio River and beside Lake Erie—even on the leeward side of a Michigan tornado. But every game Nicky and I shared had ended during an evening. Wrigley Field would change that, because the ballpark held our journey's only day games.

Ernie Banks started to call the park The Friendly Confines during the era when it lacked lights. Friendly, one legend goes, because the Cubs lost there so often that opponents felt at ease. Until 1988 the Cubs offered only daytime home games. Sentiments from those 70 years are something baseball fans revere like a first girlfriend or the big fish that didn't make it into the boat. Wrigley Field afternoons are a living reminder of how baseball began, growing out of the sport's innocent youth and into adolescence as the national pastime.

We also marked Wrigley as our pinnacle because it would echo Nicky's most crucial moment with his Little League Cubs. Just a few months earlier, his manager handed him a surprise pitching assignment, the kind a player can't worry about until he gets to the ball field. "Start today for us?" his manager asked. Steve Caskey had a big league appearance, one reason the Northwest Austin Little League loved him as a boys' manager. Caskey taught baseball. Nicky looked at me on that day and I suggested he should try the start. The test was everything I never had as a child: a chance to star before peers and strangers with physical prowess to show off new skills in a sport. I wanted him to feel the chance to achieve beyond his own dreams, to do something he wasn't sure was possible. I didn't want him to play safe like I often did, burnishing my anxiety and worrying what people would think. I wanted him to take the ball.

He escaped with his first three outs allowing only two runs, and his team got them all back in their half of that frame as well as two more. They presented him with a lead. But when he took the mound in the second, Nicky began a process that started to make him Nick, getting his ego cut but cauterizing the wound with a gutty second effort.

He saw his fastballs go wide. The stuff he put over the plate got hit. Then he took a hit off the foot and wanted to sit down. His pride wouldn't allow it, however. He finished the inning without allowing a fifth and tying run to score. A few tears flowed off his proud cheeks as he looked down at the rubber, riding himself harder than any opposing batter hammered his heater.

In the stands, I squirmed. The hothouse flower of sports, the pitcher, is a tough starring role. It demands concentration without analysis. It requires courage and guileless belief in yourself. A bit of amnesia is useful, especially when you've been hit hard just a quarter-hour earlier. These are just the kinds of things a dad needs, too.

Nicky developed his pitching amnesia under duress and found the forgetting useful on the mound during his final inning as a starter. His team rallied behind him for a few sparkling plays to push through a 1-2-3 inning. He walked off with the Little League limit of 55 pitches under his belt after those three innings.

While I was on my way to Wrigley with him, I looked over and saw his Cubs jersey and knew he'd have more time on life's mounds, standing in a starring role, trying and failing at first. He'd stand on my shoulders and be better than me. He'd succeed at last because he had the ability to try. Nicky reached into himself on the mound that day to satisfy his manager, but the real winner was the boy who was becoming Nick. He learned that a second effort after failure could bring another kind of success: the winning of respect for your ability to try again.

By the time we headed to Wrigley I'd kept us safe and avoided a meltdown—so far. But considering how fast we drove to arrive for our first game at Wrigley, that last goal was not assured.

We drove the flat turnpike roads between Toledo and Chicago, and no straighter or less interesting miles can be found anywhere except the extremes of West Texas. Turnpikes were made to be sped through, and Nicky was never going to tell me I was going too fast. That was my responsibility—mine and the Indiana Highway Patrol's.

One stalwart patrolman made his day part of ours about 35 miles outside of South Bend. I can't be sure if Nicky's presence in my front seat helped or harmed our cause, but a youngster wearing a Cubs jersey had some impact. I hoped that Patrol Officer Wilkers was not a White Sox fan. I couldn't claim to follow either team, since I was wearing my Reds jersey.

We sat by the side of the road waiting for the officer to run our license plate and scrutinize my license. We were from Texas, yes, but Nicky was a Cubs fan, wearing his jersey. When the officer's eyebrows rose at that, I laid it on. My son was showing me where real baseball was played, we had seats we'd saved up for, it was everybody's first time at the Friendly Confines, on and on. I was talking faster than my wheels had been spinning. I only had enough self-awareness to remember that nobody ever argued their way out of a turnpike ticket. But you could argue your way into jail.

"Shit-shit-shit," I said as I saw the officer chattering into his radio. I didn't have priors, had my son in the seat next to me, and we were dressed for a game. This should be easy, right? Just write me the ticket and send me on the way with a scolding.

But it's a long time sitting at the side of the road when you're late, and I was just a few stray sentences from a meltdown. There was not much of a chance of Nicky ever catching fire from the flamethrower of my anger. I just had to keep my torch unlit for the highway cops, too.

"Mr. Seybold," he said as he returned to my window. I saw him pull out his pad and felt my heart soar. A $118 ticket should not have made anyone's heart glad. But it would keep us on the road. "I shouldn't be doing this," he went on, "but I can see that you're on your way to something you think is more important. Safety is my job, though, and it had better be yours. For that boy's sake."

A direct challenge to my fatherhood. I could feel the rush to my chest, the breathing more shallow, a buzz in the air. A meltdown was at my lips. He was wrong, and after my custody agreement I didn't want anyone else in the law telling me how to parent my boy. I could say too much and then trigger my ultimate disgrace.

"Thank you, officer," I said, struggling to push all of the sarcasm out of my voice.

Nicky started to giggle. He looked down when I glared at him, but I couldn't hold his glance. I stared down at my hands on the wheel, gripping the faux leather while the patrolman teed off on Nicky's cue. "That's right, son. He's a funny man, but you need to keep him in line."

"He's a Reds fan," Nicky said. "What can you expect?"

The officer laughed. "You're good, kid." He offered the citation pad to me and told me where to sign. "Have a good time at the game, son." He tore off the ticket. "And you, be safe."

We pulled away and Nicky started to laugh in a bolt of nerves. "Well, now we have a reason to be late."

"Yes, Officer Wilkers."

"Did you say whiskers, boy?" Nicky put on his best Smokey from *Smokey and the Bandit*. I laughed, pouring out an explosion of sound in relief. I heard my boy's voice beside me and thanked my good luck I hadn't been busted this time for being the angry guy.

The clock on the Sunbird's dashboard didn't deliver anything comic, though. We were behind schedule but could still make it for First Pitch, if nothing else screwed things up.

I AM A PRISONER OF MY EXPECTATIONS, and Wrigley Field was not likely to let me escape. I knew it as the third-oldest baseball field in the world and the only one with ivy on its outfield walls. It was called the Friendly Confines, for crying out loud. If you can't have a great time at Wrigley and you're a baseball fan, ardent as we both were that year—well, you'd never be happy. The perfect game was sure to live there.

When we finally got to Chicago, my expectations were crouched in a shadow. The hotel clerk at the Radisson caught a load of my mania about getting to the ballpark on time.

"Can you hurry it up? I mean, we're trying to get to the Cubs game."

"I wish I could make it faster, sir. It's our computers."

"I bet you tell that to everybody." I turned away after the clerk stared at his keys and the screen of a terminal that looked older than either of us. I looked at my watch for the fifth time and saw Nicky had wandered off to the edge of the lobby bar, where the Cubs pregame show was playing.

"How far to the ballpark?"

The clerk looked up, and I saw him swallow. Weak.

"It's about five miles. Take you about twenty minutes with traffic."

"Yeah, well, I'm not driving. C'mon, you know what I mean." My voice rose up to rattle over the other guests' heads, the ones trying to check out at 12:30, instead of check in. The heads turned and watched me, but it wasn't my fault. It was the damn hotel.

After the sixth time checking my watch, I slapped the counter. "You don't get it, do you? I drove 1,700 miles to take my little boy to this Cubs game. So do your job and get us out of here. We've got someplace to go." I turned and saw Nicky watching me, but when our eyes met he looked away, glancing to the pregame on the TV. Harry Carey, soul of the Cubs, was on the screen.

"So how about it? How's that computer now?" The lobby around me turned quiet, even though there were more than a dozen people in line.

"There you go, sir." He looked up, his jaw tight. "How many keys for you?"

"The little boy is eleven, so you figure it out. One will be plenty."

"I understand." He swiped the key through the machine. Frowning, he swiped it again.

"Now what?"

"Just an extra minute."

"You could calm down, fella." The voice behind me belonged to a man with a grey brush cut and a Cubs jersey on.

"Mind your own business. You can see I'm in a hurry, right?"

The brush cut stepped up to me, standing a full head taller. "Look, we're all in a hurry. But you're being a…"

"What?"

The clerk cleared his throat. "There you go, sir. Will you need help with your luggage?"

"I don't have time for that. We're leaving." I snatched my keys off the counter, spun, and stepped hard around Mr. Brush Cut.

"Have a nice day, buddy," he said. "If you can."

I had more to say to the man, even while my heart was roaring and my pulse pounding in my ears. We weren't going to make the start of the game anyway. I was sure of that. I gathered up Nicky and headed for the elevator.

He walked with me quietly, looking at his shoes. "What was the problem there, Dad?"

"Hotels, you know? Sometimes they're nitwits at the desk."

"Nitwits?"

"Stupid. Not trained enough."

"Okay, I guess." We got into the elevator and he reached across and put an arm around my waist. "Thanks for this, for all of it," he said. "I mean, we're gonna see the Cubbies."

"Not on time, I bet." His face didn't fall as much as I expected.

"We got there okay, Randy and me. It'll be okay, I think."

Randy probably didn't have a meltdown like I had. I felt my heartbeat slow and the fog of regret creep through my chest. "Well, maybe we'll get there on time, you know? At least we're taking the L, so we don't have to park."

When the elevator popped open we trotted down the hall and I swiped the room card, holding my breath. The click rang out like a starting bell. I could get us to the park on time, whatever it took. A week on the road to get here. I was in command now, stepping up to the plate.

IT WAS TIME TO HAVE FUN. I had to remind myself of this while we rushed to the ballpark, plowing along the eleven blocks to the station for the L. Chicago's transit is named for the part of the line that circles the city overhead, an elevated railway. I eventually found the L station up north of Loyola, but there was nothing elevated about the station. There's only one

L, right? I parked the Sunbird, threw up the top with its motor grinding way too slow, then scooped up the Bibb Falk. Oh wait, the tickets. I zipped open my brown leather butt-pack twice, checking for the keys that were actually in my pocket. Once we got to the edge of the train platform, I tapped that pocket again, just to make sure.

I pushed our $2 at the ticket seller in the window. Great, another clerk.

"What zone?"

"We're going to Wrigley."

He pushed the tickets back at me and said, "This one's gonna be a busy line today."

I looked over at Nicky, who was flipping through the pages of the Bibb Falk we'd already carried all those miles.

"How busy?"

"It's game day. Whaddya expect?"

What did I expect? Probably too much. I expected us to have an easy time finding the Wrigley stop on the L. I expected our seats to not be in the burning July sun through the whole game. I expected that we would get to the ballpark early enough to see batting practice. I expected to have enough cash on hand to get us lunch at the park. And yeah, I expected the game to be good—and close. All those pieces had to line up for this to be perfect, I told myself. The dream was bent around my expectations by now. I stood on the L platform and hoped we were getting on the right train.

There's a right way to have fun, and my attitude definitely wasn't it. Then I saw Nicky watching me, and I remembered to laugh. "Cool, huh?"

"It's gonna be great, Dad. Wait until you see it."

"You think so?" I pushed away the fact that I wasn't introducing Wrigley to him. Not like Tiger Stadium or Cedar Point or the Jake in Cleveland, not like Riverfront or Kaufmann in Kansas City. This Saturday was like our first night a week earlier, where he showed me the Rangers' ballpark, the place his stepdad showed him first. I took a breath and remembered that this was the first time I would see him revel in Wrigley. That could be a piece of something perfect.

"You're gonna love it, Dad. I guarantee." He blew a bubble from the gum he'd been chewing and I saw that little reliever on the mound, the one who had been cool under pressure. I took a deep breath and smelled Chicago and the grease of the train rails. I reached over and wrapped my arm around him to hug him.

"Did you take the L when you got there last time?"

"No, we took a cab."

"Foolproof, huh?"

"Okay, I guess. We didn't get to ride the L, though."

"First time for everything, then."

"Yeah." He pulled down his Cubs cap. "Your first time on the L?"

"Yup. We're doing this part together for the first time." The wind moved onto the platform as the train rolled in. "Great day for a ballgame."

Nicky grinned and added, "Let's play two."

It was the Banks' catchphrase about doubleheaders from the '60s, the years when I was a boy with no idea about subways, day games, or driving like a maniac over the turnpike on the day of a game. Banks used the phrase to describe things being so perfect on a Wrigley day that the team ought to play a doubleheader. We would be getting two day games at Wrigley. If things weren't perfect today, there'd always be tomorrow.

I ENTERED THE TRAIN CAR TRYING TO BE THE FATHER WHO made fun happen while watching over his son. It wasn't a high bar to reach for most people. Fatherhood was sometimes a stretch for me, though, stepping up from the spot where I started with Nicky. I was not eager to be a dad at first. I just wanted my first wife to get pregnant as a remedy for an illness. Once Nicky was on his way, I whiffed at my chance to shower her with thrill about fatherhood.

We were working together in the small-town paper in Burnet, Texas, my second job in journalism and her first. We'd only been together for three months, and each time she had her period the pain would send her to bed. Endometriosis, I learned it was called. I could only watch a few times as that condition attacked the woman I loved.

One way out was pregnancy. At the cottage on the lake where we lived during the workweek, she explained that carrying a baby can mean an end to the endo. I heard it as, "If we get pregnant, this will probably go away."

"So let's do it," I said.

"Make a baby?" She took a drag on her cigarette.

"Seems logical to me."

"But it's a baby."

"And then you'll feel better."

"Maybe. I can't guarantee anything."

"No, I don't want a guarantee. I just don't want to have to watch you in pain every month."

"You're sure about this?"

She surprised me. Because she'd written a play for children's theater, I figured being a parent would be an easy challenge for her to meet. As for me, I hadn't grown into young manhood counting the days until someone could call me Dad. A life as a dad was just a chance to screw up, or make a mistake everybody would have to pay for a long time. My dad did that. I'd be a lover, I'd be a husband, sure. But a dad?

Making a baby is romantic, though. "We're making a baby," we'd say as we tumbled onto the small double bed in that cottage, lifting our feet off a floor that the cottage owners had covered with plastic turf. We lived in a vacation home, a getaway place we rented by the month without a lease. It felt more like a honeymoon than anything else. I thought of her as my forever love, because all of my loves were supposed to be forever. No mistakes. I could envision my days as a husband, even though I was not one yet. We hadn't married, but we were making a baby so she could get well.

All was not well with me on the afternoon she brought me the happy news. She was happy, full of the rush of expectations and dreams and passions rising on the event. Parenthood, at last. But for me, parenthood— no, fatherhood—was not the thing I'd pursued. For a fellow who got good marks in biology and physics, I was flunking an obvious test.

There's only one chance to make magic out of that moment your partner tells you she's expecting for the first time.

"We're pregnant," she told me at our newspaper's wood-paneled office. "Isn't that great?" She gave me a fat pitch of emotion to swing at, a ball of feelings anyone could connect with. Except me, in that moment of surprise that should not have been so surprising.

"Already? So soon?"

"What do you mean, so soon?" She lit a cigarette out of habit, a practice that she'd now have to cast away.

I fumbled for an answer. "It's only been two months."

"It only takes once when you're in love." I couldn't think of anything to say, a rare state for me. She exhaled and I saw her size up the man and the moment in front of her. "We wanted this."

"But I'm not ready. I mean, it's too soon."

"I can't believe I'm hearing that from you. This was your idea."

"For you to get pregnant, sure."

"You didn't think I was going to carry this baby and not deliver it, did you?"

"No, I'm Catholic, for God's sake. But I didn't think—"

"Didn't think at all, I can see." The office lights were now shining in her eyes. She blinked and looked down. Her voice shook. "It's on its way, Ron. Our child. And I hope you can learn to love it."

"Oh, I can," I said. "I don't need to learn that."

But what I genuinely wanted to learn was how to hold onto my piece of her love. A baby, how do we make room for that love? We were so new then, a couple as fresh as the Texas wildflowers that grew in the bar-ditches along the roads to our cottage. Being a father meant it wasn't about just the love I needed. Life was about us and our baby as well. I had only the memories of my dad's failures to guide me; I ascribed all the successes in my childhood to my mother. Mom would be proud of this parenthood. I had to find a way to love this child and put my entitlement aside. I was being written into a lineup of love that was bigger than just me.

Missing her fat pitch of joy over parenthood was the first of my sins in our relationship. That swing-and-a-miss would ultimately lead to the beginning of the end of every day life as a dad. I faced a father's duty before Nicky was even born, sometimes reluctant and frozen by anxiety. My dad might've felt the same. My fright of not getting it right lingered after that moment of first pregnant bliss arrived. Even before Nicky was born, I was holding myself to an unreasonable standard of perfection.

ON MY SUNNY DAY IN CHICAGO WE HELD A STRAP and a handrail, me reaching all the way up and Nicky grabbing the steel bar in the car. I was groping for perfection. We stood all the way on the 37-block ride to Wrigley. The car rocked and squeaked like an antique roller coaster, but soon enough it started to climb out of the neighborhood called Lincolnwood. And with the elevation of the tracks, my mood swung back upward. I knew nothing about mood swings at the time. Nothing good could last forever, so I didn't let myself wallow in the joy that poured through the windows of the train car.

Nothing from the crowd around us suggested we'd be at our seats, or even inside, for First Pitch. Being in place had become a ritual to pursue, something to calm my anxiety. Real fans show up on time and stay until the final out. I had four months to get ready for this Wrigley moment and I was coming in behind in the count. I wasn't experienced enough to know that getting an 11-year-old into a 1:20 game in Wrigley, when you start in Toledo that morning, was going to be unlikely. It was my second Saturday fantasy of getting a boy into gear early.

I scanned the walls of the train car for a system map and looked for a stop called Wrigley. It would be one of two, but I wasn't sure which. The car slowed, the wheels squealed, and the doors rolled open at the first stop. Crowds dressed in the red and blue of the Cubs poured out, a stream of happiness and a wave of laughter that I let myself ride upon. Had to be this stop. I held Nicky's hand so as not to lose him, and he pulled me along as if he knew where we were going.

The crowd carried us in a game day stream, two Texas fellas floating like leaves on a current. The train platform led to three flights of stairs, wood and concrete swaying a little with the slap of shoes on steps. We walked through Wrigleyville, the neighborhood around the park, where a hopeful light played down on a stellar afternoon.

Then we were on the street, and then I saw the entrance, that red and white sign that looked like it was built in the '20s. It had a small electric sign underneath saying Cincinnati Reds, 1:10 pm. I'd even gotten the start time wrong.

I clutched the tickets in one hand and gripped Nicky's with the other as we swelled up to the gates. They tore our paper and handed me the stubs. Our seats were in the 300s, so we had to walk up the ramps to get to those heights. I could hear the crowd's cheers after the music stopped. The first

pitch must be sailing over the plate, a roar going up when the ump called a strike against the Reds. One more moment I'd miss.

"Guess that was a strike," Nicky said when he heard the cheer. We pushed through the crowd on the ramp, the sounds of footsteps rippling up a wave of eager climbing.

"Just the first pitch," I said, but I couldn't look at him. "First of many." Shelter your disappointment, Dad. It will be a fun day no matter what. You drove a week to get here.

"There will be more strikes, Dad. It's the Reds, you know."

"Oh, so it's that way," I said, pushing a smile into my tone. "Then who's in first place today? I don't think it's your Cubs." We were already tossing taunts, like my brother and I did as fans of those 1972 Series rivals the Reds and the A's.

"We'll see," he said. "I'm hungry. How about you?"

It was lunchtime, for sure, but after we slid into our seats I got my first panorama of Wrigley. It remains a pocket-sized park, and it was the coziest one we'd seen. But beyond those acres of outfield grass, the scoreboard—one still operated by men who moved inside it, posting by hand the numbers in small windows—was topped by a grove of flagpoles, one for each division across both leagues. A flag for every team was attached to each division's lanyard. Those pennants ruffled from the lowly Brewers on the bottom to my Reds at the top. Twenty-eight flags, waffling in a breeze that beat its way in from Lake Michigan. Our seats were far above the field, but the dividend was a view of the lake, that vast inland sea of china blue. The game action 80 feet below was less vivid, but the vista from Wrigley's top deck could be sold for the price of a ticket.

A few batters in, before the Reds even finished taking their swings, my stomach grumbled. A scoreless inning ended and we plowed out of our seats—"excuse me, pardon me, thanks"—toward the upper concourse concessions. It was a sunny day up there with the wind riffling pages of our Bibb Falk and lifting popcorn kernels out of classic red and white striped boxes all around us.

The hot dogs were alleged to be extraordinary. Chicago was a meatpacking place, after all. These were not brats, not links, not kielbasa, just dogs served up Wrigley-style. Celery relish, salt, kraut, and mustard if you wanted. I ordered a couple for us and fished out $12. Welcome to Wrigley's prices, cash-only, like everything in a 1994 ballpark. After four hours on the turnpike and boiling my way through the Dan Ryan Expressway, nothing could have tasted better. We eased back into our seats and I felt the snap of that casing in my mouth. That dog performed like one in a circus.

I savored the dog while it carried me for a moment into my Midwest boyhood. A meal wasn't real unless it had meat. Pimento loaf, baloney, liver, corned beef. Chops, ribs, shanks, Swiss steak. Chuck, mostly, and never a breath of ribeye or prime rib for us—those were meats for the table at rich Aunt Lottie's home on River Road. Stew meat was big on our menu, cooked in the blue-and-white cornflower Corningware dishes on the stovetop until it was lean. Dad made it by adding Bisquick gravy, calling it all shit on a shingle. That gave us license to say shit all night, until Mom would put a stop to it.

Wherever Nicky did his swearing, it was out of my earshot. He had nothing to rebel against on his visits, because I laid down few laws. There was little time for discipline. The multi-syllable kind of profanity I learned from Dad had not crossed Nicky's lips on our entire trip—not through the blistering heat of our Texas departure, hustling away from Cincinnati's sketchy hotel, or the calamity of the tornado on the way to Detroit. I pelted out profanities during the worst of that time on the Dan Ryan, so Nicky might've joined in. But neither of us were the kind of fan who swore at the ballpark.

His first Wrigley visit, with his stepdad, might have given him a head-to-tail tour of English. He said his seats were in the bleachers with the Bums, men who made a religion out of swearing at the enemy outfielders patrolling the grass. I imagined the straight-arrow engineer of Nicky's stepdad sitting alongside his stepson, Randy going rogue and giggling while the Bums barked at opponents. I could mimic the Simpsons back and forth with Nicky, but swearing was too close to the angry guy behavior I was sealing off in my past.

No matter what happened after that day's final inning, one of our teams would leave the park a winner. The Wrigley games would be the final time our teams would battle on the trip. The cheering and taunting would rise up between us inning after inning, after each out or run, with every straining catch at first or error at short. If my brother and I were at a game like this, we'd want to prove we were right about whose team was best. We'd get loud, because we were raised by loud people.

When I replay that first Wrigley game, I remember how little happened at the plate. The afternoon was a day of sticky Great Lakes midsummer air, the light eventually slanting into Wrigley after the sun fell behind the grandstand. The blue skies gave way after a while to high clouds. Cracker Jack and root beer and Dr. Pepper followed our hot dogs, all of it trailed by soft pretzels with mustard slathered onto the wax paper for dipping. We leaned into seat arms crafted of metal that could brace a battleship. The seats in front of us grazed against our knees. In that palace of nostalgia, nobody brushed up against anything as modern as a cup holder.

We saw no ball leave the field over those ivy-covered walls. Nicky's scoring reported that bases were stolen. On and on and on the Cubs came to the plate, got on base, but failed to score. My yellowed clipping from the *Chicago Sun-Times* tells me 15 men were left on base, the most of any game on our trip. After seven innings our teams were scoreless. A game was unfolding without runs, one that only true fans would crave. Each of the strikeouts that would end the top or bottom of an inning—nine in all—triggered cheers from Chicago fans, or moans when Reds pitchers would fan the last Cub batter. Bean-balls. Dropped third strikes. The blazing-fast Deion Sanders, entering as a pinch hitter, then cut down on a stolen base attempt.

The crowd's steady disappointment rose up in grumbles. I savored the drama of a close game. Every missed Cubs chance meant my team might pull out a win. In the eighth the Cubs turned an error, a single and two walks into a run and eked ahead 1-0. The Bibb Falk was already thick with marks, inning after inning of hits, walks, and errors. The stubby pencil we got with our $5 program was worn to its nub. It was 1-0 at the top the ninth with the Reds at the plate, Chicago on the verge of a win in front of a jammed park. The air buzzed with an electric sound like a chorus of box fans in the windows of a muggy Great Lakes night.

That was a Cubs team with Mark Grace and Sammy Sosa, but its unheralded Kevin Foster was pitching a gem for the home team. "He's gonna toss a complete game," Nicky said, nudging me and grinning. "And shut out you guys." Like every avid fan, we talked about our teams using words like "we" and "us," and "you guys" for the fans of any opponent.

"We'll see," I remember saying, because there are few Nicky arguments in my fuzzy recollection. "We've still got three outs left to tie it."

"But only three hits today from you guys," Nicky said. "Pathetic."

"We'll see."

Nobody had pitched a complete game during our first seven nights of baseball. The three-hitter from Foster was almost complete going into the ninth, with 24 of 27 outs already recorded. Then the Reds tied it as he tried to close out the game. The sound of 41,000 people swearing at once followed a Reds double from Larkin that plated the tying run. The Cubs failed to shut the door on a win in the final inning. Then in their last chance to win in regulation, the Cubs' final ground ball died in the first baseman's glove in the bottom of the ninth.

"Extras," Nicky said.

"Bonus baseball," I answered, like a call and reply from my Catholic boyhood. We'd already had three hours. The good fortune was enough to prove to myself that I was a great dad, not the angry guy who tormented his family into a divorce. But the play at Wrigley was not over. I held my joy at bay, believing a win would seal this sign of happiness to come. I needed proof. It had to be my team leaving with the W after I'd already accepted two Rangers losses with grace.

We drifted downstairs into the concourses below our deck. Into the tenth, the eleventh, and the twelfth, each team hit but did not score. The Cubs put together three singles in a row in the tenth but somehow fell short of the winning run. The gods were giving me what seemed like a perfect day. In the hours after I entered Wrigley with Nicky I felt no fear, just a beam of light on my face and Nicky's shoulders. That perfect day came to a close when I marked down the Reds' winning run in the thirteenth on a pinch-hit single that sealed the game. Reds 3, Cubs 1.

Four hours and 17 minutes, that yellowed *Sun-Times* clipping reports, delivered 48 at-bats for the home team. Even the power of Sammy Sosa couldn't end things for the Cubs. He cracked out four singles including a two-out hit that gave the Cubs their first lead, but nothing left the park. Best of all, we watched a game between our teams that was tied for twelve innings. Close games move at their own pace, a clock that nobody cares about and never runs out. It was a Saturday with deep dish pizza on our horizon, after all. We got the longest game of 1994 played at Wrigley, enjoying the season's biggest crowd.

The marks in the Bibb Falk show we shared the scoring, with Nicky's easy scrawl on the Cubs side and my constrained letters on the Reds half of the page. I scored it as a come from behind win after the day which unfolded with a patrol officer, as well as my scorn, fury, and hurry on the turnpike, the hotel, and the L. We spilled out from Wrigley onto Addison Avenue, a street bustling with taxis and vendors hawking Cubs shirts and jerseys. Its taverns and bars were already brimming with loud-talking drinkers.

"Some finish," I said, walking alongside Nicky on a sidewalk jammed with fans. We picked our way across pavement spattered with pigeon crap, crushed soda cups, and wadded up cigarette wrappers.

"We'll get ya tomorrow, Dad."

"Tomorrow, yeah. We get one tomorrow, too." In that moment, a second day at the mythic ballpark seemed like an impossible treasure. Some people only get one such game in their lives. We'd have two. I already had a Reds win in my pocket. Anybody could win tomorrow and it would taste sweet. We had pizza for our supper, Uno's. In the afterglow of an epic game the city's best-known pie was a revelation and a promise kept. We didn't expect it to be as thick and decadent as it was, while we watched the crowd ordering slices from the take away window.

We rode back toward the hotel's suburb on the L. Outside the car's windows, the sun was fading behind the western side of Chicago's skyline. The voices in the swaying car talked about the extra innings—a hard luck loss, one said. I wore my Reds jersey with pride but no swagger. The relief of our success and safety washed over me. Chicago was a messy, foreign place, biggest town of our trip, but it didn't harm us. It painted our day with memories. Nicky stared out the train window as the Howard Station and the L's parking lot came up around us.

"Game time tomorrow, 1:10," I said as we left the train.

"How about we get there at 11? BP, you know."

Batting practice was a ritual we hadn't enjoyed since Cleveland. On the seventh day of the week, we'd be rested while entering the ballpark. "Tomorrow then, for BP."

WRIGLEY SUNDAY SERVICE
Reds vs. Cubs
Wrigley Field
Sunday, July 24

If my trip was a race around a diamond of proof I was a good dad, then the Sunday that we woke in Chicago we were tagging up at third, ready to head toward home after that Wrigley game. Yes, there was one more stop in St. Louis, but this Sunday was the day when we'd slingshot back toward Texas. We'd leave town after nine innings and another Uno's pizza, bedding down at some indeterminate point south of Chicagoland. The day didn't start with a long car ride. We only had to take the L—an effort less than an hour's drive to a park like in Detroit, or a full day crossing the Plains to make First Pitch at Kansas City. We could arrive early and watch batting practice. This would be a second afternoon at the place I dreamed of while I'd trotted across Nicky's Little League field.

The game would be a day game after a day game, one thing that makes Wrigley Field so magic. Sundays offer day games all over the majors to get fans home in time to start their workweeks. But much of Saturday's Major League Baseball is played at night. Weekends with those double day games at Wrigley are a tribute to its lights-free roots. On our Sunday, we watched baseball under the same light that illuminated the Cubs for more than 70 years: sunlight.

The players were stretching and warming up when we walked down to the front row rails. On a sun-swept Sunday, we were arriving at our church of baseball. We had our game rituals as surely as any I'd served as an altar boy at Nicky's age. In St. John the Baptist church I held the polished brass platen under communicants' chins while they accepted the card-like wafers of communion. Inside the Wrigley gates, we held our souvenir program and scorecard and stubby pencil. In church, the faithful would rise up after they crossed themselves, the wafer dissolving even as they walked back to their pews. At Wrigley, we made our walk to the gift shop with no rush before the first pitch. In church, I'd walk the rail with the priest as he passed out the hosts. At Wrigley, we crowded the first-row rail of the field to watch batting practice. We lingered at that wall, unlike those Catholics who hurried up off their knees and back to their pews after communion. On this Sunday, we had ample time to commune with Wrigley.

It was also our first game where I already knew the geography of the ballpark. The concessions were no mystery, and I did not worry whether we'd be on time or know the correct entrance for our seats. We'd done better for seating than the prior day's game, getting a pair in the lower level and on the first-base side. By that morning I felt as competent as the sitcom fathers on TV shows I watched when I was Nicky's age.

As always, the events on the field were captured on the Bibb Falk. A scorebook belongs on a boy's lap. Or his father's, sitting close beside him in a ballpark jammed with fans. But the scorebook is best of all when it's traded back and forth across the nine innings of a game. On a good day in a weekend at Wrigley Field, the sunlight played down on the pages of our Bibb Falk, bouncing off the whiteness and sharpening the blue lines that held our notes about the game, They were written in ink by Sunday—a more assured hand, and when I'd get it wrong in ink it would be obvious.

Mistakes are something to correct in life, and we did our corrections right in the moment on the Bibb Falk.

"Not a pop fly, but a ground ball for an out," he'd say, taking it back from me during a change of the inning.

"Okay, mark it 4-3," I'd say. It was the most common play in the game, ground ball and the throw to first. Pretty much close enough, 4-3 was the note we'd make whenever we'd miss a play. Something imperfect would unfold on our scorebook.

"Dad, scratch out that line you drew from first base to second. That guy was caught stealing." The scorebook became the place we shared our mistakes. We corrected each other during the ballgame, the same kind of revisions that an epic story gets during retellings.

We sweated in the July sun, so the moisture left its mark on the pages of the Bibb Falk. It was the evidence we were at the game in person, sitting close. Nicky's handwriting and notes rested alongside mine. The pages we filled on that day were a marker of us writing together. Nicky might never write as a passion, but on that afternoon with the scorebook passed between us, we shared a story. I hoped I might retell it to make it more epic, even with its mistakes.

I was ready to risk a mistake, and so I let Nicky explore a ballpark by himself. He knew Wrigley better than I did, after all. Although he was 11, I'd put my hand on his shoulder as we'd moved through all those ballpark crowds. I did not want to lose him. We navigated those packed concourses of the weekend without the safety of cell phones, never mind smartphones. If we had been separated, the safety net would have been the stadium police. In 67 innings of baseball up to that day, I'd never heard an announcement about a lost child. I didn't want to be the father of the first. Keeping Nicky in view helped me feel safe and in control.

Baseball that's played on any afternoon can be a low-scoring affair. Saturday's game had been tied at 1-1 at the end of nine full innings. Sunday's game had little scoring. But my, what those two teams showed us in the field. A catch deep in the ivy in left field led off the Cubs' fielding in the first. That was more than vegetation out in the park—that was an obstacle. Both teams completed a rundown between first and second to erase a base runner. The Cubs were not impressed with the speed of Deion Sanders; the two-sport star nearly got picked off and then was out in a rundown. Shawon Dunston of the Cubs was called out on runner interference crossing first, another fine point of baseball to study. "Being fast to first isn't enough if you don't stay inside the base path," I said to Nicky. Making the trip was my way of getting back inside the base paths, a series of days where I avoided getting called out on anger.

The Sunday was 79 and sunny in the final game of a series that broke Chicago attendance records. The afternoon was burnished with ballpark memories that Wrigley colored as its own: Queen's "We Will Rock You," played for the first time I'd ever heard it on an organ. The crowd broke out in "YMCA," complete with antics of making the letters as we sang, and Nicky added, "I like it when they let us choose the song." The Wrigley crowd made its choice by applause at the song choices spelled out on the tiny electronic scoreboard underneath the legendary one in center. The opposite of a Jumbotron, that board was, just three lines high.

The Reds managed only five hits, scattering ground balls that the Cubs scooped up. Jim Bullinger threw eight masterful innings, relying on his fielders to produce 20 of his 24 outs. Team play was leading to a shutout. It became evident that Nicky was going to get a win for his team that afternoon. When the seventh inning ended with the Cubs up 3-0, I asked the baseball gods to send my son the victory. I already had my Reds win from the day before. Perfect: we'd both get a win at Wrigley.

By the eighth he was sitting across the aisle from the seats we'd crept into, that habit of fans who can't afford the close-up seats. Harry Carey had led us in "Take Me Out to the Ball Game," a tradition that was no more indelible than something I captured with a candid picture.

For the first time since we left, Nicky was talking to a boy his own age. My son had been my charge, a delightful mission, but I'd also been a parent responsible for his safety. So I'd held him close. Once the Cubs held a safe lead, Nicky was sharing his Stone Temple Pilots knowledge with a boy he'd only just met. In the last few innings, as the ushers looked the other way when we moved down into close-up seats, Nicky sat beside that boy like all pre-teens, youngsters who converse without looking at each other. I watched from across the aisle, seeing Nicky grow easier with his new friend, the Cubs erasing the Reds as the game wound down. I tried not to let it sting too much that my last handful of Wrigley moments were ones Nicky didn't share with me. I went toward the concession stand to buy Cracker Jack for all of us.

I'd look at him over my shoulder after every other row, then spotted a vendor walking the aisles. I paid him with the last $20 bill I'd brought, and I saw Nicky throwing back his head and laughing at something his new pal was saying. They shared talk that only two 11-year-olds could enjoy. I pulled my plastic camera from my fanny pack and started snapping, a string of pictures not aimed at the field and the game, but at a couple of young fans. It grew quieter, the crowd murmuring with that sound you only hear in the oldest of ballparks, an echo off the steel beams overhead and bouncing off piers stenciled with "Watch Out for Batted Balls." Then Nicky looked over his shoulder and smiled at me, got up with his friend and moved down into empty seats even closer to home plate. I waved and moved down a little as well. I kept my distance. I was enjoying a new moment of being a parent watching a couple of boys under his wing. A trusted man, I imagined to myself, secure in his fatherhood. So this is what it felt like.

I removed my cap, already dotted with pins from Texas and Kansas City, from Cincinnati, Cleveland, and Detroit. I held the Cracker Jack boxes under my arm. I was waiting for that gap when every conversation lags before I approached their seats. Until that moment, I settled into an empty seat and rested, certain I had photos to prove he was having fun. I made friends with the happiness a father feels when he watches his son at play on his own. It was a break in my vigilance. I felt my breath come easier.

On the way back to the hotel, I looked around the L car at other fathers with sons. I wondered how many of those men might be dads of divorce, engineering a too-special Sunday with kids they didn't live with anymore. My whole trip could be colored in that sharp light, we Custody Dads who over-praise, over-spend, and over-commit to things like every inning of two weeks of games. By keeping my summertime pitches across the plate of Nicky's heart, I was righting my wrongs and forgiving my sins. This was absolution my dad never seemed to need. He didn't watch us as we played at playgrounds or in the street outside our front door. I was going to watch more avidly than he did. The steady quiet of the Cubs' easy win let Dad's silences sweep back into me.

DAD'S AIR OF MYSTERY PROTECTED HIM FROM THE LABEL he feared, that of being a fraud. He developed a story about himself but told it like playing a jigsaw puzzle. Bits at a time eked out: a World War II tale about rescues of pilots in the Pacific, one with "a face so tore up it looked like goo when we fished him out of the water." His tale of such rescues from an unnamed aircraft carrier was a secondhand story; Dad's service papers showed he didn't leave the States during two years of Navy service. But he held onto the story as one of his most courageous hours, a story that I didn't want to doubt until long after he died. This was the tale of a hero, or at least a man doing something brave. Like a surprising number of his stories, it was probably a bald lie.

Another was his win in that fight with a neighborhood kid. He shared the story to give me a model to stand up for myself against being bullied during grade school, but he told it like he was a David in the shadow of some Depression-era Goliath. He knew enough to reveal such mysteries with care. He handicapped us as listeners to win a wager, a bet that his stories could survive any close scrutiny.

His mystery trapped him, though. He did not see the solitary confinement which he sentenced himself to by sticking to that slim volume of stories. His friends accepted him as a book with few original chapters. I met these men who knew him better than I did during the few card parties thrown in our house, or on nights when we were dropped off for babysitting on couples' nights out. One sitter, two sets of kids, all for economy. Dad's friends could improvise stories from their lives. No question that we ever asked Dad's work friend Ed Perry went unanswered, however foolish Mr. Perry's reply sounded. Dad was a commenter and a critic, not an improviser. The account of his life closed up like a bank vault when I'd ask him about his mother, the grandma I never knew.

Polishing his playlist of tales, my dad told them like stand-up comic routines. His bits relied on a style of delivery, not insights. Insightful George Carlin was no favorite. But George Jessel brought out dad's belly laugh. The release of his barked guffaw played like a fanfare as he lounged on the couch, watching comedies unspool across the black and white tube on the Zenith. The release of dad's laughter was so sudden and welcome in that it spiked the mysterious punch he served every day. Dad wore the mantle of parental king like he was some kind of regent, looking over his shoulder for someone more capable to assume his throne. He feared being imperfect and could rage over the prospect of being discovered.

In time I learned to avoid the standard questions some kids ask: the ones about Dad's early loves or worst mistake, any unfulfilled but still hopeful dream, or the wealth of his family. I had no idea about how Dad's father earned a medical degree. Cancer took Pippi before I was born. His memory was something Mom revered more than Dad seemed to. She brought baggage to her marriage with Dad, being a divorcee with a son in tow. She got respect from Pippi. The tone in Mom's voice when she'd laud Pippi suggested he was her protector. Like my own fears of becoming a father after my wife got pregnant, Mom said Pippi chided Dad for fearing the prospect of fatherhood.

"So what if you do get her pregnant?" Pippi asked him. "It's what men do." Pippi could quell that revolt of Dad's worries. On Dad's worst days, I wanted the legend of Pippi around.

On Dad's best days he was like me, choosing something showy to demonstrate his love. He'd cook something precious in the kitchen, like fudge, in an era when men left that kind of work to their wives. When Dad was at the stove, it was as special as anything that I hoped our Sunday at Wrigley would feel to Nicky.

I only ever saw Dad prepare four dishes, but one marvel was evening pancakes, made to order in the sizes we requested. He pretended to work at a breakfast grill. No batch was complete without silver dollar cakes. He dropped them between steaming disks of regulation-sized ones, grinning and then glancing back to see if we were watching. His wrist flipped each of these cookie-sized cakes onto its back. He cooked to entertain us, never as an obligation.

The fudge was a different kind of event, though. Mom never made it, or his peanut brittle he cooked, or the hard candy dripped into tinfoil that he let us fold into deep grooves, each waiting for the melted syrupy sugar he'd colored. She held back, I suspect, to give him his chances to shine gently. He made the fudge a group effort, teaching all of us how to keep beating the syrupy melted sugar until it was just short of hard candy. I was younger than Nicky when I stood at the Kenmore white porcelain stove, my brother alongside me, my sister on a chair, taking our places at stirring. Somehow he'd enforce turns, barking each of us away until it was my little sister's turn to finish it off with tiny strokes of the worn wooden spoon. His tough directions ensured that his kids who were already high-strung would whip the spoon while he'd say, "Don't let it get too hard now," or "Faster, pull it away from the fire." Then there would come a "That's enough," and my sister would slow down but not stop. He'd just stand behind her, a gentle man with his only daughter, reaching around her to slow the spoon, lifting away the double boiler he held for her, then tipping the fudge into a Pyrex dish.

Rules fell away for how much dessert we could eat on fudge nights. The way Dad smiled, the rare aspect of his happiness, seemed to show his need for our glee as we set upon the fudge. The smell of the cooling cocoa preceded our sounds of combat over who'd get the biggest piece. Mom would let the skirmishes unreel while she watched her husband smile at his children. I made something they crave, he might have been thinking.

Such gifts were tied up with his obsession for perfection. There was always blame at hand for any mistake. But there were mistakes, and then there was the abuse I passed along from one generation to the next. Every time I roared at Nicky's mom in an argument, or the times I snapped at my little boy in a flash of anger, I echoed what I'd learned. I needed absolution for those sins. I'd whip my anxiety into a hard candy of anger. When the cheers rose up at the game's end at Wrigley, though, I smelled something sweet.

I TURNED HOMEWARD WITH MY ROLLS OF FILM bearing evidence of Nicky's unchecked joy. We saw both our teams win at the Wrigley games. It would never be more perfect. I gave myself a moment to mourn Wrigley's passing, glass-half-empty fellow that I am. I'd tasted perfect from those afternoon glasses and still I was thirsty for more. The miles we crossed took on a gloom like the ones when I'd take Nicky home after visitation Sundays.

We were leaving Chicago for a hotel in the city's outskirts, a bit more affordable. Every dollar counted, and I was counting every dollar. Tomorrow we'd drive to St. Louis. My relentless itinerary meant the sun still wouldn't set on us twice in the same Major League city. I drove away from Chicago tipsy with sentiment, bathed in the nostalgia of the almost-oldest place in baseball. Our day games were behind us. We were rounding third and more than halfway home, sitting beside each other and sated with victories.

Dad sat a little too close on the last night we were in each other's company. He'd probably held me that close in his lap while we watched TV, but on our final night together we sat at the kitchen table and played cards. Poker, the game he'd taught me using the adult-sized container of red, blue and white plastic chips. Seybolds talked to each other while they played cards. Dad and I had a stack of each color as high as our fist. The pile between us was less than a dozen. He held his cards tighter than an acrobat's grip.

Dad had already played out his hand in life, the mistakes and the oversights that anybody with kids can make. He hadn't learned much from the mistakes, not even as much as he taught me about how often you could expect a royal flush, what it meant to check on a bet, or how many face cards were in a deck. We played for an hour that night, him quieter than I'd ever seen and more silent than I remembered.

I already had my bag packed and the car was gassed up. The army post in Texas was a long way from Ohio, and it was winter, so the driving would be slow. Dad looked defeated, but not while we were betting and drawing and filling out straights and flushes. The defeat came afterwards, or maybe it was surrender. He didn't have battles to fight anymore with me. The lightning in his eyes was gone and his thunder was absent, too.

He wore the bathrobe he'd been in throughout the holiday, except for one night he was soldering up a project in his workshop. Most of his time he spent in the TV room or the kitchen. He was watching me, but not with that prodding look I knew too well. He was asking a question with his eyes. Would I remember, he asked me finally—would I remember him after I left?

I could feel the answer he wanted from me and I gave it. Of course I would. How could a guy forget his father? I knew the answer to my own question about remembering, those reasons a young man might forget because of knife-point arguments and rules I chafed at because I was a teenager. I wanted to let all of that go. I began to do it when he asked me about being remembered. At the door I hugged him and he clasped me tight, like those poker cards of his. In that minute I was in his arms again on that couch watching TV, the old comics on the variety shows making him laugh. Then Dad told me that he would always remember me, too.

It was a funny thing to say to a son who was only going back to the Army, but I forgave him for that as well. He was a little confused that night, I guessed, maybe a little tipsy like he had been in the old days. I didn't take his rambling about memories to be a forecast about his ending. I forgave him like he forgave me for the recent past between us.

When I hugged him he hugged me back in a way I had not felt before. He whispered in my ear, "I'm so scared, Ronny." He said it in a voice that rattled me during my first half hour on the road driving away.

Because I overthrew my dad during my teenaged years, the ones close to his death, I gave myself blame about his suicide. Surely I had a duty as his son to love him, hard as that was to do sometimes. I accepted his belief that bad things happen because someone makes errors. In the years after my divorce, I blamed my behavior in that first marriage, even while I pointed out my ex-wife's faults. The roots of my cruelty in that marriage were as much a mystery as anything about Dad's family ties and why he broke them with us.

DAD'S FOB ALWAYS HELD KEYS TO CRUCIAL ITEMS of ownership like houses and cars, but the Sunbird I drove was just a rental, temporary like our trip's moments of perfect. I wanted our perfection to become as permanent as the fob. The keys swung a little in the car's ignition. The fob was an object infused with his essence. Whenever I wanted to conjure Dad, it smelled like his grip, all certain and subtle, the grasp of someone with the skills for the detailed work he called electronics. He would tinker at his work-like passions throughout the evenings. Then we had to go to bed and we'd go kiss him good night in his workshop. His fob swung in the Sunbird like those kisses.

As I sped away from Chicago, I was already wondering how long any single day's perfection could last. How could I find the next? Sunday was the most perfect day for a Wrigley ballgame, but it played out in seats I chose months in advance. Our hotel was a short and well-planned drive from an L station. Luck delivered no part of that weekend's perfection. My control was like the snaps on that key ring on that fob. I fingered it while I drove. Snapping up this trip's promise was supposed to lead me to a more perfect place. As we left Chicago, somehow it seemed like the road was leading me away from perfect.

PRAYING FOR BETTER
Mets vs. Cardinals
Busch Stadium, St. Louis
Monday, July 25

Nothing was ever going to match those weekend afternoons at Wrigley Field. I was as certain as the ink on our Triptik's pages to St. Louis, routing our road that rolled away from Chicago's outskirts. Interstate 55 would carry us to the banks of the Mississippi and the Cardinals' ballpark, Busch Stadium. Tucked away in my butt-pack was our final pair of major league tickets. Neither of us were fans of the Cardinals, or their opponents that night, the Mets. The stadium had nothing much to recommend it, either. Busch was another of those misbegotten ballparks built as a concrete ring suitable for football or baseball. The Cardinals and Mets would play at the last fresh ballpark on our homeward route. It would be new to us, but promised only artificial turf and more concrete than a ballpark needed. It was simply on our way home.

We rode the Interstate alongside travelers who looked like they couldn't have been farther away from baseball. A group just as famous as the Cubs had played in Chicago during our weekend. I knew nothing about the concerts the Grateful Dead played in McCormick Hall, but now their fans the Dead Heads were following the group to its next gig, much like we were following the schedule of major leaguers. Nicky and I took a break in a couple of rest stops along the highway. We were treated to the company of kids in long hair, VW micro-buses, and the scent of a burning weed that Nicky didn't recognize as fast as I did.

"Hey Dad, what's that smell?" At a rest stop he wandered closer to the grassy pet-pooping area.

"What smell?"

He scrunched his boy's nose, tanned from almost a dozen days on the road. "That. Oh wait, I know." He broke into a grin that he shot at me like a ball hit hard down the third base line.

I handled the hot shot as best as I could. "Yeah, it's weed. You smell it a lot at concerts. They're Dead Heads."

"From the Grateful Dead. So they're grateful for…"

"The music, I guess." We broke into laughter and looked at each other to begin the Simpsons line. "So now," I started.

"…Let us never speak of it again."

"What is this Dead Head bus of which you speak?" I said, playing at changing the subject. Another line from the scripts of the Simpsons, where there was wisdom to inform any circumstance. Or a wisecrack to wrap around it.

A couple of cans of soda later from the rest stop's machine, we pulled away, riding behind a micro-bus. As we passed it, Nicky waved and toasted the Dead Heads, leaning out the window with his soda can. He'd already blasted through seven *Goosebumps* books and was taking his rightful place as a fellow traveler, not just my playmate.

St. Louis was not like Chicago's crush of crowds. The ballgame was on a list of endangered evenings. Nobody could be sure how much of the season would be played out. The drumbeat of the oncoming strike was loud.

We lugged our bags up to a nice Radisson room, then stood at the window as storm clouds rolled over the city. We'd go to the park, of course. We had tickets and it hadn't started raining yet. Throughout a week in the Midwest, only the Detroit thunderstorm had rattled our trip. A single storm across eleven days of a Midwestern July was sort of a miracle. I sent up a prayer of thanks that we'd finish our schedule without any rainouts. We'd be able to record the trip's final First Pitch in our Bibb Falk.

We found our best moment right at the start. When the Cardinals ran to their positions on the field, Ozzie Smith did his classic somersault and backflip, leaving his feet on a run and landing at shortstop as he took his position. Ozzie was nearly 40 and on his way to the Hall of Fame. But his team managed only one run that night while the Mets' Bret Saberhagen pitched a complete game.

During that season of heavy hitting, nine complete innings from any pitcher was rare. Saberhagen was on his way to throwing for the full 27 outs with a healthy mix of ground balls, pop flies, and strikeouts. Infielders and outfielders made his complete game a reality. After the fourth inning, he held the Mets to only three men on base. Fly balls fell into fielders' gloves eight times, plays we could at least see from our seats out on the front row of Busch's upper deck in center field. The game was full of three-up, three down innings. Ozzie's somersault was the highlight of a tepid night. The game proceeded quickly, though, that speedy pace of low-hitting games.

The rains began after the fourth. A genuine downpour like that tornado in Detroit might have chased us up into the concourses. Instead, St. Louis delivered a steady drizzle, a misting rain that was enough to get us damp but not hard enough to stop play. The temperature fell throughout the game and I did not want to abandon our front row. I logged each play with care in the now-damp Bibb Falk. We sat through the full nine innings because I would never leave a ballgame before the last out—not even if I was not a fan of either team, sitting too far away to beg for an autograph or snag a foul ball, or worn down from 2,700 miles of driving over eleven days. These were all true, but I had a ritual to preserve.

There was tidy and error-free baseball to admire amid the absence of offense. Saberhagen and the Mets were denying hits and runs for more than two and a half hours. In Busch we watched the best pitching of any scheduled game on the trip. The 7-1 game tested the purity of my baseball love. Ardent fans feel they need no offense to watch. I needed someone to root for, even while I watched a complete game. There were only 102 such games in all of the strike-shortened season of 1994, so finding one across our small sample of games was rare. But who needed a lot of fly balls and grounders in a light rain?

As the light showers fell, I pondered what we might do for three more days until our Friday return to Austin. I craved every one of my days with Nicky. I had Wrigley and its glories in my pocket. St. Louis was a quiet coda of the Mets and Cardinals slogging through the dying innings of a season that looked sure to be stopped by a strike. I had to admit that anything beyond Game 9 at Busch might expose the risk of an overtired parent snapping at his son.

The next day, we plowed through the Tuesday miles of Missouri. Like the last time we traveled across the state, there was no ballgame waiting to anticipate and imagine that night. The Burger King driveway at Port Giradeau dumped us onto the road to a monument. With our Whoppers in hand, we made our way to a park on the Mississippi, one marking the Trail of Tears march of people who I called Indians as a boy. Nicky hacked away at a stick with a pen knife I bought him at the park's gift shop. We chipped in a few minutes of a halfhearted game of catch, but the July heat caught up with us in a steamy Missouri afternoon.

On the drive away from the park, the car seemed to grow quieter with every exit sign we whipped past. I glanced at one that looked just as tilted as that sign Dad veered toward on that manic vacation turn. He wasn't lost on that day he commanded the family station wagon. Just five years farther down his road, though, he'd started to turn away from any route to peace. He believed he was dying even before his heart attack upended his life. During the years before I moved out, he roared about the house, barking about shooting pains "those damn doctors can't find." That attack forced him into an early retirement, rousting him from the sanctuary of his job. He hadn't been fired—he was shit-canned, as he'd call it. That departure was preceded by a desperate stab at disability pay. As an electrical engineer, his heart's circuit was broken without his job. His sons were serving in the Army thousands of miles away. My mom and sister learned to keep their distance from a man who knew all the express lanes toward melancholy.

Dad shot himself in a room he remodeled from the cinderblock out. When we were just toddlers, he added the yellow waterproof paint to keep the stone walls from sweating. Later there was the asphalt linoleum from Armstrong Tile, rolls as big as a mini fridge that he spread out and glued down, perhaps by the time I was in kindergarten. Six basement windows were scattered along the tops of walls that he and I paneled together one weekend afternoon while I was still new at being a teenaged son. He was seeking rituals to share, the kind I was wrapping around the baseball with Nicky.

Those basement windows delivered daylight, but never a fresh breeze, because he never opened them. By the day Dad died down there, he'd also closed up his sense of hope. If he felt sick on one day, he was certain that he'd be as bad or worse the next. It was an argument he was destined to win.

I tried to push away that basement image as I sped up to pass a semi on the Arkansas road. Fathers at knife-point with sons, dog shit as a mean prank: fatherhood could go that badly. A father could sit in judgment, a seat on a great divide between a daddy and a boy. Dad and I gave up trying to bridge our divide. He was compulsive about his judging, though, and turned that habit onto himself once there were no sons around. Unable to blame his sorrows on his family, he turned his anger onto his own heart.

The sun remained behind clouds while Nicky and I rolled toward the suburbs of Little Rock. The overcast afternoon light led me to picturing the colors during Dad's last day. The light on the highway was warm enough to see, but not bright enough to bring bright color to the world.

I don't know exactly what that basement looked like on that afternoon he died. I know little about the morning he spent by himself, either. I can see him, though, still in his bathrobe by 2, the garment wrapped across the boxers that we knew as Dad's underwear. Their waistband didn't strain over his belly anymore. He'd lost weight because he didn't eat much over his last weeks. Dad had tipped into depression. The slip would be fatal.

He might have shuffled across the linoleum floor in the mock-leather slippers Mom gave him for an anniversary gift. He'd pull his records out of a cabinet he built himself and coated with Formica, first one album and then another, looking at each but unsure what to play. Barry Sadler's *The Ballad of the Green Berets* eventually spun on the turntable. "Fighting soldiers from the sky, fearless men, who jump and die." Maybe Dad thought about his sons who were away in service while those lyrics tumbled out of the massive speakers he'd built. Dying that day would not be fearless for him.

The Green Berets must have led to Hank Williams and on to other records whose grooves held more woe than hope. The sun crept enough to slant light through those tiny windows along the tops of the walls. He listened for movement upstairs and heard nothing. His wife would be at work until 3. He left the record cabinet door open and pushed through his workshop door, his hand running across the knotty pine that he'd sanded and shellacked. Then his hand rested on another piece of wood, the stock of the lightest weapon in the house. He taught me to shoot with a .22 rifle. His .22 pistol would be no problem for him to train on himself. Compulsive to the last, he took his time oiling and loading it and found that he wanted to pray. Dad's prayer may have been for something better to be waiting beyond his very hard moment at hand. Nothing more to do here, so move along, he said to himself. Buck Owens was wailing to cover the shot.

Later, when that white vacation station wagon rolled into the driveway and the storm door creaked at the landing atop the basement stairs, Mom slipped into the kitchen with paper grocery sacks. There was a sound coming from the basement's stereo, the click of a record needle rubbing against an LP label. Dad wouldn't put up with that for long. Mom came down the stairs to see if he was standing or fallen with another heart attack. She discovered him and his fatal gunshot wound, his body slumped on our leftover maroon couch in the rec room. The phone in the basement was disconnected, so she had to bolt up the stairs to call Toledo's Rescue Squad.

I only got a bulletin about the event, reported over a pay phone at the barracks in Texas. I asked Mom if she was sure he was dead. "Daddy shot himself," she'd told me. An accident? "Shot himself" was not precise enough. I was finding my way toward the new truth that my father was gone. Around my grief, I breathed a secret relief. I was escaping his critique, his judgment and doubts about life's prospects—my prospects, as well as his own. I don't remember asking Mom why he did it. She had little to share about his thoughts. He'd descended from his random hellfire into a Sphinx in the months at the end.

Holding the black phone receiver on that spring day, my conventions shattered about how to grieve. Someone you love dies and you are supposed to weep, or maybe wail, letting the sorrow boil up so people can see your steam of anguish. The heat wasn't there for me that afternoon. I wished for it, felt the top of my head tingle. I was light-headed, maybe, although not so much that I couldn't stay on my feet through Mom's call. The yellow of the barracks' bricks seemed to shimmer once I hung up.

I asked my First Sergeant if I could get emergency leave and he said yes, of course. He seemed to know what my family emergency was from that first moment he'd told me to call my mother. I asked how much leave and he said, "Whatever you need, soldier." He was a tall man with a slight beer bulge and hair as dark as his skin. His face fell to an at-ease pose while we talked, one I'd rarely seen. I had my duty to do in Ohio. I was expected to hand over my own time for grieving and go comfort my mom.

In the years that followed, I learned to label his suicide as the ultimate failure of a father. Divorce was a gentler failure, I reminded myself while I glanced over at my sleeping boy. There's a prayer of redemption when a father can stay in the field of the game of life. You can take more chances in the field. I had fielded my chances safely on the trip. I learned not to let anger seep into my game over the past eleven days. The wrong turn in KC where I steered us into danger. Being pulled over on the Indiana Turnpike. At the hotel in Chicago, with a chance of raging into a shouting match with a stranger, an act that could have blotted out the joy. Dad's suicide did exactly that, blotting out the good that might have come out of our relationship, then staining it with all of the bad.

Staying alive to steal away from the anxieties of an unsure fatherhood might be redemption. To rescue myself from Dad's failures, I was learning to be a better father. I had more than a prayer of success. Becoming Nicky's dad could be my way of shaking free from the past.

AFTER ANOTHER HOUR ON THE ROAD, I saw Nicky fast asleep against the door of the Sunbird, his hair askew like the roadside weed patches we rolled past all that day. The AC was on stun, but he seemed to be sweating anyway. We didn't have a destination, just my need to stop driving. Forrest City was upon us by 5, and the AAA Guide didn't show a better motel prospect for more than another hour's drive.

We pulled into a Best Western parking lot and Nicky didn't wake up as I went inside to get us a room. I felt a chill coming back to the car. I figured it was just a lack of plans and no ballgame to warm us for the night. Then I saw Nicky's face. It was ashen and warm to the touch.

"Dad, I'm not feeling so good."

"What do you mean? Where?" More information was going to make things better, I figured.

"I dunno. My gut hurts."

"No more KFC for us," I said. "But let's get into the room." If he was going to be sick, it'd be better for everybody for it to happen outside of the Sunbird. We would have to ride in that car tomorrow.

Inside the room he just fell back on the bed and then curled up, his tennis shoes still on, wrapping his jacket around him. "I'm cold," he said, and I switched off the window unit of the AC next to his bed.

"Maybe you should just take a nap," I said, pulling off his shoes and laying the polyester bedspread over him. He was sweaty and cold at the same time, and that could only mean something like the flu. No, it meant the flu, but I didn't want to admit it.

"My head hurts. I'm sore."

"It's okay, Babbo." His name from his days as a sleeping baby I carried on my shoulder. "I'll get you something to eat… I mean, for your head." I tried to take a breath and push back panic. He was going to need me to be a real parent now, not just Custody Dad.

He closed his eyes. "Okay," he squeaked out, and then the sound of a pre-teen's snore floated into the room. Should I leave him alone while I fetched, what, aspirin, right? And he needed something like juice to drink. Soup, sure. How would I do that in a motel that didn't even have a room safe, let alone a microwave? He hadn't been out of my sight in more than a week, except for a few times here and there in ballpark gift shops. I wrestled with leaving him in the room while I went for his remedies, or waiting until he woke again.

After the sun started to set, I realized I had to find a drug store as close as I could to the motel, plus get something healthier than Dr. Pepper into him. He rolled over and said, "I'm gonna be sick." I got the trash can under his chin just in time. He rolled onto his back and I put him on his side, got the washcloth and dabbed at his chin.

I had a little while—and I didn't know how long for sure—to find whatever I could to take care of a fellow who once again looked like a little boy, tender and vulnerable in his sleep. Nicky had been sick at times when he was supposed to visit me, but usually his mother canceled those visits before they started. He'd come down with something a few times on my watch, but I wasn't solo on that duty. At home I had Dottie to help everybody feel better.

On my own, I was much better at imagining the worst. While I drove through the town, the car felt desolate without him beside me for the first time in more than a week. My empty-seat rides at the end of our weekend visitations began to haunt me, and I felt a familiar depression rising up.

Finding a grocery was a task the AAA guidebooks failed to assist. The clerk at the front desk could not tell me how to get to a store that sold aspirin, at least not with any directions I could recall in my fright. I drove the streets of Forrest City looking at my watch at every stoplight, searching for a Walgreens or whatever they'd call a drug store in that tiny burg. Citgo gas, Ace Hardware, Dairy Queen. Like every small town. The street lights were infrequent and made the road dim. If Nicky was sick now, would he be worse in the morning? Dozens of hours of my planning across all those states didn't include a first aid kit, a plan for any emergency room and insurance card—or experience to know when to worry and when not to.

In a blink I thought of Ozzie Smith, diving across his shoulder the night before. He tumbled and snared a hard liner that would've been a hit into the gap. How did he do something that looked so hard? I can't say for sure, but I might have brushed up against the thought that parenting looked hard to the inexperienced man. Maybe it could look that way in the faded and foreign light of Forrest City.

I drove and multiplied the prospect of doom. If we went to an emergency room, would it lead to a hospital stay? I'd have to call his mom then, because we'd be certain to be late coming home from our trip. Since I used judgment as the rudder for the course of my life, I figured my ex-wife would also be quick to judge. I feared I'd hear about Nicky getting sick, if it turned for the worse. I was running across the outfield of my dilemma, eyeing a shot of a baseball dropping toward me, hoping I could make the catch.

I raced back to the motel room with aspirin and Sunny D, the only liquid reminiscent of juice that I could find in the Circle K convenience store. Standing in line at the checkout, I could conjure up a disapproving tone in his mom's voice. Leaving an 11-year-old in a motel room by himself wasn't something a real parent would do. I had my own fears about his safety, though, and I had to admit that feeling this fear might be what real parents do, too. And since I was doing it, maybe I was really parenting. Worthy of it, anyway.

My three little bottles of Sunny D and a container of generic aspirin rode in a white sack until I was back in the room with my boy. He was out cold and still warm. I nudged him awake, made him sit up and take the pills and swallow a few gulps of juice. But then he dozed back off. I sat there with my gut clenching and the light completely gone from the Arkansas sky.

In the dark I thought about Dad, the man whose fathering made our road trip possible as well as necessary. But in that motel room with Nicky, I did not think of my dad as a tender man. Sixteen years after he killed himself, Dad deserved a kinder revision of our history together, but I struggled to muster it. I listened to Nicky's quiet snores and started to believe that he'd be okay. I began to feel a lifting of the pressure off my chest, my breath slowing and deepening like my boy's. I faded off into that dreamy state that I get after a burst of panic and thought about the malady of breathing I shared with Dad. We had bad sinuses together.

ONE NIGHT DAD STOOD AT THE STOVE HOLDING A SOUP SPOON. The flame rose from the burner, just a little, and he used an eyedropper to fill the spoon. He had taken his empty peanut butter jar, tucked away under the sink, and loaded it up with tap water and two spoons of baking soda. He shook it hard, that water and soda. Then he took a tarnished soup spoon, the one I had never seen except in this use, dipped it into the jar, and then held it over the burner, well above it. Just enough to warm it, he told me. Then he drew up some of that soda water with that dropper. Out of the dropper, and down into his nose, with his head tilted back. Nasal drops were by prescription only, from his Ear, Nose and Throat doctor. This was probably the only doctor Dad didn't yell about and hate. On that night, his prescription of drops had run out.

But we always had baking soda and water. I watched this ritual of his for a few years, wearing a little awe and standing a safe distance away. I had gotten my own case of bronchitis, so I knew breathing could be tough. I told Dad that night I felt sick, too. He knew what I needed, he said. He prepared me for my treatment, standing before the stove and passing on a family remedy.

"Can't I just use the Vapo-Rub?"

"No. Not gonna help you." He shook the jar, holding it up to look at it in the yellow light over the kitchen sink until all the soda was dissolved. I looked over at Mom.

"Honey, your dad knows this stuff." I saw her watching him while his eyes were on me. He wanted to be in charge now, but why? Mom was better at this stuff. He turned to his eyedropper and filled his spoon.

"Come here," he said. I couldn't imagine how I'd inhale water. But it was not a choice. "You can't avoid this. Not if you're gonna get well," he said. He lifted the dropper to my nose. "Tilt back now."

I inhaled as he dropped. I gagged and coughed. I leaned over the white porcelain sink.

"Spit," he commanded. I hocked out something. We were sharing something serious, a ritual we established on that day. What I didn't know in that moment, or many others that followed, was that he was always a kinder man when caring for me. Not caring for me sweetly. Not any more than his own dad the doctor might have done for him. His dad was a professional who must have saved his bedside manner for his patients.

I HEARD COUGHING FROM NICKY AND I TURNED ON THE LIGHT next to him. He was sweaty, but cooler somehow. I helped him up and he used the toilet and then I put my hand on his forehead. It seemed there was a real cooling. He snatched one bottle of the Sunny D from the nightstand, edged up in bed and looked at me.

"I feel shitty," he said.

"That's it? Shitty?"

"Shitty," he said again, and gave off a little sheepish laugh. "Shitty," he chirped, a little louder.

"No, not shitty?" I asked, in mock horror.

"Oh yeah, shitty," he said. "Not even close to the bathroom, either."

I broke character for a moment. "You need to go?"

"No, I'm okay dad." As it grew quiet, with the only sound the tinny roar of semi tires out on Interstate 40, I saw him reading me. "It's okay." Then he put down the bottle and rolled back over and nodded into a fast sleep.

I sat in the chair next to his bed and put my head in my hands and thought of all the things I'd do if he'd just get better, soon. I made bargains, or offered them, but what I was seeking was experience. I sat in a small Arkansas town with a sick boy and no hope except what I could make myself. I closed my eyes and found a way to ask God to make it okay. Even when Nicky was sick in Austin, in any home, I didn't feel the tightness in my chest like that night in Arkansas. I could listen only to my voice in my head, talking about how I got myself here and blaming me in the dim light of illness. I knew how to improvise, though.

I had to admit that I prayed for Nicky to feel better in that Forrest City evening. But I told myself I only prayed to my Guardian Angel for a feeling of confidence. Maybe, I thought, a feeling like the firm touch my dad used on that night with the baking soda water and the dropper. In the dark of Arkansas with Nicky perhaps on the mend, I asked a higher power to be able to show me that much faith. Proof of angels might be beyond Arkansas, but we'd be back in our home state soon.

The next day I craved a confirmation that I'd kept Nicky safe through his feverish night. No evening of his life ever presented more of a threat to my credentials as a father. A fever, maybe even the flu? That would reflect on my competence. I did not understand that competence is the hat of authority I was driven to wear, like a chef's toque. Especially me, a man so quick to draw my sharp blade of criticism. A good chef can be trusted with a sharp knife. In the time of our road trip I was a sous chef, at best.

Nursing someone through a fever takes patience and faith. The prize I won from my patience was dawning on me while the sun broke the horizon the next morning. Nicky had come down with a one-day bug, just at the limits of how much fatherhood anxiety I could manage in the twelfth day of a road trip. Everybody felt better by sunup, Nicky in body and me in soul.

OUR ROUTE WAS RETURNING US TO TEXAS. Since nearly all Interstate roads go through Dallas, my plan was to stop there. It would bring me within hailing distance of my loving wife. I craved time with Nicky against the classic backdrop of family: wife, husband, and son.

It was not much of a mystery why I failed in my first marriage. I was angry, over-dramatic, and hunted by anxiety. I had my excuses about each of those badges. The first was a family practice of all Seybolds, something we saw as more of a style than a sin. The second I confused with passion. The last, of course, was my unnamed disorder. Then a woman entered my life to try to show me that an obsession with tidiness and order was a poor way to encourage happiness.

Dottie was my backstop for parenting. By the day Nicky and I plowed our way through the rest of the Arkansas cotton fields that lined the Interstate, we rode closer to a reunion with the woman who always assured me I was worthy of an All-Access Parenting Pass. Dottie made Parenthood 102 a continuing education course for me—no grades or judgment. After nearly two weeks apart, I craved her laughter and exuberance as much as Nicky's close contact. The woman we both called Dot was a powerful beam of sunshine that lit up my frequent gloom. Following her lead was like running downhill, arms akimbo, chortling with glee—even when a river bluff lay at the bottom of the hill. She could make going over any kind of ledge an easy thrill.

No day of my trip was complete if I didn't review my worries. At a rest stop in the fresh light of that Arkansas morning, I called Dot. With the close brush with Nicky's fever just behind me, I wanted my backstop beside me for the finale of our trip. She heard my flu night's report, a story I delivered without fright in my voice.

"Is he okay?"

"Sure he is. We're tired and sunburned, but doing fine."

"So why the call?"

"I miss you."

"I miss you too, but you'll be home today, tomorrow at the latest, right?"

"I have an idea. Meet us in Dallas. We'll do a Rangers game together."

"A game… tonight. Maybe tomorrow?" Dot was usually up for sudden fun.

"Sure, tomorrow. I guess the Rangers aren't even in town until tomorrow. Talk to Nicky about it if you want." I handed him phone and he ran through a report of our week-plus of touring. I was still striving for something more perfect, even after a park full of coasters and 85 innings of baseball. As a family of dad, stepmom, and boy, the three of us had only been to a major league game once, seeing a game in the creaky old Ranger Stadium. In the new Rangers ballpark I could reinforce the feeling that I was a reformed parent. I needed Dot in a seat beside me to complete that picture.

Nicky stopped to listen to her and I got quiet as well. "She wants to talk to you, Dad."

I thumbed through the Arlington pages of the AAA guide I'd carried to the phone. "I'll get us a nice room, one for the three of us." The word "Suites" wasn't in many motel names. But there was one, and luck blessed me that it was within 20 minutes of the Rangers ballpark and just a half-hour from the Dallas airport.

"Okay, I can do this," she said. "It sounds like you need me."

"Like oxygen."

"Well, you don't have to hold your breath. I'll get a flight. Let me go, so I can call and get a ticket for today."

In that era without online booking, this was all I could hope for. The logistics felt tricky, though. She'd have to book the flight and then I'd have to call her to get an arrival time and a gate number.

"Don't worry," she said. "It'll be coming into Love Field. All the Southwest flights do. Just look for the flights arriving from Austin when you get there. Wow, a pickup at an airport by my lover man." She was already revving up. "What should I wear for you?"

"A ball cap for tomorrow," I said, "and something soft for the evening." Nicky arched an eyebrow at this.

"Okay, white blouse, jeans, and big smile at the airport."

But which flight? I hung on, clawing for a plan, even in the middle of an improv moment. I was a fledgling improviser. Finally she said, "Just call me on your first bathroom break from the road. Really, I probably won't have left the house yet."

That sounded jumbled. Probably? "Can't you call me right back?" I looked at my watch. We should've been moving already. Dallas was still five hours away.

"Just trust it, honey. It'll work out great."

As we bore down on Texas, Nicky may have sensed I was about to drift my spotlight away from him. I justified this with every mile we drove toward Dallas. We'd shared nine baseball games across the last 12 days. One of those no-game days was at Cedar Point, too. I was tempted to add up my dollars spent, more of them than I'd planned. I'd given Nicky enough to show I was a perfect father. I totaled it up and knew, in a part of me that made the shame and the judgment, that it was a math equation where I couldn't show my work. I could point at some perfection in our Wrigley afternoons.

IN THE TERMINAL AT LOVE FIELD, I SCANNED GATE SIGNS to spot the one for Austin aircraft. Then as now, Southwest controlled almost all the gates. Dot's plane was scheduled to arrive sometime after 6, she had told me. In mid-1990s the answer to which was the correct gate came from a gate agent, not any computer-driven display board. Dot flew to meet us during the era when gate agents slid city name cards into slots, like the church hymn lineups I'd post as an altar boy.

I said a bit of a prayer for her safe arrival, beaming all the while as I kept my arm around my boy. She emerged from the taxiway flashing a smile brighter than any late afternoon flight deserved. She hugged Nicky first, gathering him into her arms in a way that made me envy how he got the first slice of her love.

But when she turned her eyes to me, she dished out pride along with a kiss that was more chaste than I expected. "I know we haven't seen each other in a while," she started.

"A long while," I said. "I've got us a suite."

"Great. I can't wait to see it." She looked over at Nicky. "Your dad's got us a suite. You'll have your own room." I drove the miles to the hotel hoping for just enough of a room to keep us intact as a family, but with enough privacy to let me catch up with my love. Parents capture such moments where they can leave their chastity at the curb. Dot grinned at Nicky and then flashed a different look at me. This was to be affection served family-style.

GAME 10

A PERFECT TEAM
California Angels vs. Texas Rangers
The Ballpark in Arlington
Thursday, July 28

On the morning of our fourteenth day, I walked to the window at the Rangers ballpark to buy day-of-game tickets for the first time in my life. It felt reckless, such fun without planning, but I was trying to learn something from my wife. Nicky wore the Stone Temple Pilots t-shirt that had been rescued from the grime monster by a washing way back in Toledo. His hair, tousled and sandy, still bore the bed-head stamp from the night he'd spent in the suite's guest bedroom. He slept late, another gift of having no driving schedule to meet. Dot took us to the ballpark, the first miles that I didn't have to drive in two weeks. We walked to the window like a real family: me and my son, along with Dot who called herself his stair-mom. Step-mother sounded too Cinderella-wicked. She made her role different by her own design.

The OPEN sign blinked over the ticket window, and I breathed a sigh. We weren't so early that we'd have to wait in the July sun. I juggled the worry of getting to the park for our impetuous tickets against a later wake-up, but eventually being early won out. In the clear, unhazed light of that morning sun, the rumba of the cars and trucks danced away from the I-30 turnpike behind us, floating over the white lines of the parking lot that led to the ticket counter.

The idea of day-of-game tickets was foreign to me. How could anybody be sure they'd get inside if they didn't buy tickets weeks in advance? The ballpark would hold more than 47,000, and I'd already seen from our first game that there's not a bad seat in the Rangers' house. But that evidence didn't reassure me completely.

We made our way across the plaza to the window. Nicky ran in front of us while we reached for each other's hand. I had endured her absence over the last two weeks, time that was joyful, a dad and his boy out playing together in a game of being perfect baseball fans. Not an inning missed. Yet in that moment, the trip felt richer with her beside me. I sniffed the air in front of the box office, seeking the scent of mustard.

I eyed that ticket window with hope. Would they have anything good I could afford? That game against the Blue Jays was nearly sold out. The Rangers were in first place and riding a six-game win streak, and this was the first home stand after a road trip. Their ace Kenny Rogers was pitching. I tasted the fresh concrete dust, the kind that takes months to settle after building a park. I felt Dot squeeze my hand, leading me toward the unplanned. Something good was coming up, she believed, always without needing a reason to do so.

I wanted to get great tickets for our grand finale. But at what price? The trip's budget was teeming with impulsive expenses. That $27 commemorative Rangers ballpark pin set from our first night was still in its box. A souvenir bat from every city, photos from the Cedar Point coaster's tunnel, all costs I carried in my head. But when I got to the window, my caution dropped. I thought about my cub reporter sports column from the day Nicky was born. *I look with longing to afternoons when we'll share third-base seats.* That was where we should sit.

There was nothing available on the lower level, so it was the upper deck for us. My heart sank. This final game wouldn't match all of the poetry of my column. I hadn't planned this game like the nine others before it. How could anything this impulsive be as good as those weekend games in Wrigley Field? I couldn't even be sure why I was still searching for a perfect game, having already anointed the Sunday afternoon in Wrigley as perfection. Possibly because Dot was with us. Upper deck would have to do for this game.

We headed away from the window, this time with three tickets in hand, to seek out lunch. At a Chili's down the road we escaped the heat. Across from me sat the two people I loved best. They believed in me out of habit, but also because they loved me. Maybe it wouldn't matter how good that night's game would be, or how special the seats were. Nicky looked like he'd found a second wind, laughing more, his smile brighter.

We dined on baby back ribs, burgers, and enough fries to make Dot think we hadn't been eating them for thirteen straight days. This meal wasn't carried away from a counter in a bag. Someone brought it to a table. There was a second adult in our party now, so I had to class it up a little—even if all the class I could afford was Chili's. There was a Chili's out at that new ballpark, too.

I was reveling in the backup the one parent gives another. I could see how much difference love could make on the road when two parents trusted each other. Mom and Dad never managed it. After all of the combat between them, and mine with Dad, I fled. My ultimate breakaway came when I joined the Army.

I became a buck private so I could study to be a professional actor. It was an odd way to pursue a life in the arts, but I believed Dad made my enlistment necessary. Even in my first summer overseas, when Dad was diminished by heart attacks, altered by electroshock therapy, and humbled by an early forced retirement, his power as a chieftain lingered with me. After my three years of service, I'd have GI Bill money for acting school. Then Dad couldn't tell me what to study.

Like many of my adventures, the Army was not what I expected. The military life would be just a supporting player to my dreams. Then my unit was sent to the mountains of Wildflicken, West Germany. Dad's son was not only away from home, but across an ocean. I didn't write. During that first summer when Dad had no work to define himself and no sons at home, he reached out to me using one thing he loved and had taught me about: a recording, in the form of letter shared on a cassette tape he mailed to me.

He'd applied a signature from his rubber stamp onto the back of the padded package. I took the envelope to the hill overlooking the German barracks where we all slept, eight soldiers to a room. The grass on the knoll was cut close after we'd swept the grounds with our sling blades that morning. My platoon leader Sgt. Stone told me I could think of every blade swing as bringing me closer to college.

I toted Dad's cassette and my portable player to the hilltop for privacy. He rambled and rumbled about life in a house that was so quiet now. A dig at my departure, or an admission that he missed me? I replayed the section and was still puzzled. Then he began to wrap up his letter and splashed out a surprise.

"Maybe that acting thing of yours is right for you," he said. "If you believe it, then you have to give it a try."

I loved him as simply as a dog loves his master in that moment. He was my dad and not a taskmaster, not with those words he sent me. I played the ending again and tears overtook me. I was forgiven, and so he was as well. I now had an ally who'd be proud of me when I would take a curtain call in front of him for the first time. He couldn't stay in the game to meet that moment, though.

We decided to take in a matinee before the game. Disney had bought part of the California Angels that year and remade the classic *Angels in the Outfield*. The Rangers were playing the Angels that night, so it seemed fitting. We sat in the theater in the same order as always: Nicky between me and Dot. The AC lulled us until the rousing finale. An angel's magic lifts an outfielder into the air for a game-saving catch. I cackled at Hollywood's fantasy.

At the Rangers' ballpark the lights played across a field still scrubby in the places where the first-season infield grass hadn't taken hold. But those beams of light wrapped the diamond in a neat bow. The scent of spilled beers and wind-blown popcorn made its way up to us. Indulging my compulsion, I compared the park to the others we'd seen. It wasn't Wrigley or The Jake or Kaufmann, all named after people, or bearing Tiger Stadium's historic double deck all the way around the park. It was ours, though, us Texans either native born like Nicky or emigrated like Dot and I. Before the first pitch I led the way for pretzels and looked over the flat-as-Legos landscapes that spread away from the upper deck's concourse. We were in a park that had no history and was so new it hadn't yet been named after a corporation.

Inside, I worked to make the park part of a personal history. With my economy camera built entirely of plastic, I snapped pictures of Nicky and my Dot together. I spotted a man in a Rangers t-shirt holding the hand of a little boy. I reached out to hand the camera to him.

"Excuse me," I said while I pulled Nicky and Dot closer. "Could you take our picture together? It's her first night here."

"No problem," he said, framing us up with the scoreboard behind us.

"Could you take it with the light from the field on us?" I knew his framing would backlight us, underexposing our faces. My dad would tell me that, his voice still with me even in the park. I wouldn't get a second chance at a picture of our first Ballpark in Arlington evening. We stood together as a blended family, my bride and boy and me, taken with arms around each other, all wearing ball caps. Mine dotted with ballpark pins. Dot's the Ranger blue. Nicky's the same hue but with his Cleveland Indians on the front. Nicky wore a Will Clark Rangers t-shirt kids giveaway. We took our seats together, looking onto that diamond where the Rangers had fallen behind during the first inning of this trip.

I settled in and measured my expectations, remembering that the failures of Texas pitching first came here against the world champs at this ballpark on the trip's start, then again in that pounding up in Cleveland. Fatherhood is about overlooking expectations, though. Setting them in place, then releasing them when things get imperfect. Kenny Rogers set down the first three batters. Jim Edmonds, the Angels' candidate for Rookie of the Year, worked the count to 3-2 and then watched Strike Three whip past him to end the inning.

The Angels came in looking bad after a half-dozen losses in a row. My fathering was built upon such history, the downward trends in my life that I was sure would continue, but continued to brush past. Rogers wasn't shaking off any of catcher Pudge Rodriguez's pitches, but I had to shake off the history of Dad's fatal failure and my loss of a perfect family after the divorce. In the second inning the Angels' best batter Chili Davis flared the first pitch into center for an out. Two-sport All Star Bo Jackson swung at a third strike. Rogers needed only five pitches to retire the side. Good hitters were going out swiftly. So much for trends. Dads need to ignore trends. Every game has the promise of being a win.

In the third, the Angels' best slugger Rex Hudler looked at a third strike. Only seven outs in, Rogers seemed to swell with confidence. He'd only gone to a Ball Three count once over the first three innings. When he needed a fly ball out he could count on Juan Rodriguez in left or the rookie Rusty Greer patrolling center. Rogers was mounting his confidence, a fathering aspect I was learning to embrace after two weeks with my son.

Rogers now had set down the complete Angels order. But hitters read a pitcher much better the second time around, so the danger was greater with the 1-2-3 batters up again for the Angels. Chad Curtis ripped the second pitch into deep center but Rusty caught it near the wall. We were building faith in Rusty's speed and his read on the ball. It was faith that put me onto the road for nine games over eleven days. Misguided faith, but dads need faith to get things moving.

So far, the Angels were perfect failures. Hudler would eventually be up again and there was no pitching around him. The Rangers' sluggers, Pudge and Gonzalez and Jose Canseco, had pumped in four runs by the fourth, but Rogers' 4-0 shutout could be undone with so much game to be played. Slugging gave the Rangers their wins that year, but long balls took them away, too. They had a pockmarked infield as well. Those errors committed in the first game I'd endured had proved the grass could be tricky. A dad can't avoid something that's already shaken their parenting, though. They've got to face it head on. In the fifth, J.T. Snow lifted his best shot of the night, a fly ball that landed in Greer's glove in center. Rogers was eating innings with right and centerfield outs, putting the ball in play. Strikeouts are personal wins; balls in play require a team effort. Rogers couldn't pitch around the Angels, but he was teasing the corners for called strikes.

By the time the sweltering night slipped below 90, the Angels' futility was complete up to that moment. The Bibb Falk got passed around, from my lap to Nicky's and back. He was balancing it on his knees, with his feet resting on the seat in front of him. The big crowd made the night even hotter, but the breeze in the air brought a blessing as the wind shifted from left field to right. I looked up at the scoreboard above the Home Run Porch. The lights glared over that board and I started to scan its numbers. Zeros, so many, for these last-place Angels. I felt a creep of electricity in my legs, damp against the green plastic of my chair.

"Hey," I said to Nicky, "let me see that scorebook."

"Sure," he said, still affable during our enforced sweltering. As he handed it across, he looked up at the board.

I watched him sizing up the board. "See it?"

"A no-no, yeah. No hitter, wow."

"There's more." I handed him the book back.

"No. Hey, no walks for them."

"No errors, either," I said in the quietest voice I could manage.

"A perfecto," he said.

"What? Oh my," said my bride.

"Perfect game. So far."

Perfect games are so rare in Major League Baseball they might as well be two-headed cows born in a blizzard. They call them perfectos, and on that night they'd only been achieved 13 times over more than 210,000 games across 125 years of baseball. A perfect game is nine innings of absolute order, but it's impossible to find on a schedule. Fate and good fortune rules who can be in the stands. One team sends one man after another after another to the plate. They all fail to reach base safely. Twenty-seven up, twenty-seven down—in a perfecto the batters all get no farther than first—and any who even make it there get thrown out. Some do not leave home plate, stopped by strikeouts. None of the nine fielders makes an error on such a night of perfection.

The odds of being in our seats to see one—well, you need six decimal places. A perfecto is so uncommon that by that night there were three times as many US Presidents elected as perfect games played. We were watching a total absence of offense. On an impulse, I'd bought seats for nine innings of baseball that had a growing chance to be a perfect game.

Every one of the other hundreds of thousands of games started out with the same chance. They're all perfect for awhile. An official perfect game emerges over a long cycle of actions, nurtured by luck and daring those odds. I was taking my own long shot at two weeks of happiness using eleven hotel nights to see eight ballparks—all of which I'd never tried to find in thick traffic or the dark of the night. Every check-in, every fill-up, every Quarter-Pounder we discovered in the right place at a time that fit our schedule, every parking space or subway train caught, they were all individual plays in our larger game. Two weeks of road tripping with Nicky might amount to a string of disappointments as the experience fell short of my expectation. Because when the mustard is too spicy or the game is played in a drizzle or your team doesn't win, that's not perfect.

I thought we'd found perfection in Chicago at Wrigley. The Friendly Confines was my exacting destination, the turn-back point for our journey. Wrigley was planned, something I could reach for—and then later on, burnish like a cup pulled down off a mantel.

Being in those hot seats at the Ballpark in Arlington was something far different. The baseball gods were giving me a tease, a hint this trip could end on an even higher note. It was something I didn't dare wish for, but also a thing I desired more than anything. A perfect game would be a historic sign that I was meant to be more than a weekend dad. A ballgame even better than Nicky's very first trip to Wrigley with his stepdad. No pressure there, for me—just come home with a perfect game, so you can call it a perfect trip with your son.

Once a game is more than halfway over and one team has squeezed out no hits, or even taken a base on a walk or errors, the focus tightens on what remains. It takes 27 outs in a row to make a perfect game. After we marked down the first 15 on our scorebook, counting every pitch and marking every play, I started to look ahead at the nearly impossible back half of the game. Just a single "ball four, take your base" could spoil perfection. Rangers pitching had been hammered all year long, giving up more runs than any team in that season. Perfection was too much to expect as they went on to the field for the sixth.

For the second time that night, Rogers faced Hudler. He pounded out a fly ball, this one to right center, a long way out. Greer met it at the end of the outfield. Luck was in play, the good fortune a father must count on when the outcome is unsure. I was an unsure father, searching for a sign I'd be better suited than Dad was to parenting. In the bottom of the sixth the Rangers started to set up in the classic dugout seating during a no-hitter, every player sitting away from Rogers. He had 18 straight outs and needed nine more. Without a ball four, a bloop hit, or an error, he'd be perfect.

Rogers had thrown a complete game earlier in the season, during his last start in Toronto. He lost 3-2. He'd struck out eight but gave up two homers. There was nothing to suggest he was due for anything better, toting his swollen 4.32 ERA onto the mound on our night. We didn't buy tickets to see Kenny Rogers. I only hoped for a win from my team before our road trip ended.

By the seventh the walks became crucial. Nicky called out the count after each pitch to Chad Curtis and Spike Owen. "Ball three," he said in a little jab, needling me about Rogers walking his tightrope toward perfection.

"Here comes something over the plate," I said. The count was full. Curtis slapped the pitch in the spot between third and short. "Gawd," I said, "there it goes." Dean Palmer got in front of it, somehow, and threw out Curtis by a step.

"Close one, Dad."

"He's got it," I said. "You know he has." Unreasonable devotion should be in every dad's tool belt, the sandpaper that takes off the rough edges of reality. Owen then worked Rogers to another full count, testing my devotion to the prospect of perfection. Another fly ball to Gonzalez, then another strikeout of the rookie Edmonds. Six more outs remained.

Major league parks get louder as a pitcher's complete-game shutout comes together. Unlike the raucous noise of those shutouts, in a perfecto the sound of the game can wane between outs until it's as solemn as a Sunday in church. The notes of the hymns become strikeout calls from the umpire and the pop of balls into fielder's gloves. Each crack of a bat becomes a minor chord that threatens defeat.

The energy of our crowd, desperate to will away the Angels' offense, echoed my effort of driving all the miles that led to that night. The road to any perfect game gets ever-quieter along its route. We endured the Rangers at-bats in the seventh. "All that matters is the top of the innings," I said. Nicky grinned and drained his Dr. Pepper. We thirsted for history.

In a complete game a starter holds on for nine innings, tiring with every pitch. In a perfect game the cheers for him churn into a buzz of whispers about an event nobody wants to name out loud, for fear of a jinx. They had announced the official strike lock-out date earlier in the day. The anticipation and desperate desires began to fold back on me. This would be no perfect season. The three of us kept looking at each other, even as a miracle flickered on the diamond below.

The eighth was like the last two innings before it, built around a fly ball to Gonzalez. Jackson again, slugging at .500, swung at a third strike and missed. Snow followed with a strikeout looking. Facing those hitters twice already meant Rogers had to be crafty. He was in his second full season as a starter and sixth overall. At 29, he was a veteran capable of guile. It's a quality a father can use to accomplish whatever's needed when a child threatens to overwhelm him.

"Only thirteen, before now," I finally said aloud while the Rangers went to the dugout at the bottom of the eighth, "have ever been played."

"Now just three more outs," Nicky replied, the call-and-answer of our faith in the game's promise.

We'd made our marks so far on the pages of a scorebook that already held family history. Nicky's championship relief performance was just ten pages back. In that season, the other dads stood on his Little League field during that game, coaching at first and third. A few were helping in the dugout. Not me. I was a professional watcher, an ex-sportswriter. My sports column introduced Nicky to the world on one perfect day. In the Ballpark in Arlington, I was finally living out that Sports Shots dream I conjured on the day he was born.

Inside that Bibb Falk, every mark that year was a love note to my son. They'd be as private as any song, because to find their true meaning I read between the lines. 1994 was the first full year I worked for myself. I went freelance to take jobs that were the lines between the measures of my love song to Nicky.

In the moonlight of that Arlington evening, though, I had to force myself to make a mark in the Bibb Falk as the final inning began. I couldn't take my eyes off the field. Losing a perfect game in the ninth, at the very end, would be the most painful. Hudler led off, and the best Angels batter whiffed at two pitches for strikes. He stood one swing away from a strikeout, or one swing away from a deep fly ball like he'd hit in his previous at-bat. I dreaded a repeat of that, because in the sixth he took Rusty Greer right to the warning track. Then I heard a sharp crack of Hudler's bat, a sound that lifted all eyes to the outfield. I feared the worst, as always. That hit was a frozen rope, dropping too fast.

Away in center field, Greer wasn't even playing his regular position. He wasn't a speedy centerfielder, and usually played over in right. He launched himself in a gallop toward the ball. He was too far from it. It was going to fall for a hit and ruin everything. Rusty ran for the catch, but he was running out of time. Then he leapt, his body flying off the ground and moving horizontal as he stretched his glove toward the ball.

Nearly every perfect game has a moment when all looks lost. Greer ran with courage, knowing the perfecto could be lost on his effort. Dads need courage to attempt what they've never done before. I left my job to begin a freelance life, a way to protect and direct the time I could devote to Nicky. On a night with hot dog wrappers under our feet, some angel in the Texas outfield lifted Rusty off of his feet. He seemed to float like the fielder in the matinee Disney movie. Greer speared the ball with his glove and skidded on his belly, rescuing perfection for a moment. The crowd exploded. Just two to go.

A quick grounder to short took us to the last batter, Rogers' final challenge. It came from the bottom of the order in Gary Disarcina. He lifted a slow fly to Greer, who this time needed no help from any angel. He camped under the ball, watching it all the way into his glove. And in a split second, the park transformed into a place of bedlam.

After those innings of hushed and hopeful quiet, our cheers sprayed off the green outfield walls and tens of thousands of seat backs, now empty while the crowd stood as one. A blizzard of camera flashes captured the scoreboard with its historic numbers, all zeroes in a row along the line score for the Angels. Zeroes for a hero standing in the center of that diamond before us. Rogers needed a team behind him, as I did. Nothing could bring me and my son and my wife to a perfect game except luck and the pursuit of love. No one, not man or boy or woman among those 47,183 fans was leaving that ballpark. Cheers rained down onto the field, floating off the Home Run Porch and cascading from Chili's Front Row Grill in right.

In an era before smartphones, we recorded the images with cameras like the cardboard Funbox, a Kodak with built-in film that was sold in that ballpark. Then I thought to push the button on my Radio Shack recorder. The sound mounted from one moment to the next. Drinks tipped over at the thunder of tens of thousands of pounding feet. Nicky's oversized Dr. Pepper cup spilled under our seats, sprinkling its ice into the next row. A mob of players swarmed the mound, throwing their caps and leaping on each other, a blur of blue stockings and white jerseys. The dust from their celebration rose far above that scrubby infield and into the light. We could breathe out loud at last, after an hour of holding it in while praying that the almost impossible perfection might finally arrive. Standing on our seats to cheer together, I high-fived Nicky.

That night gave me more than perfection. I uncovered a shiny faith in the ideal of a blended family, bonded tighter because of a baseball game, a thing of no lasting consequence to some parents. I took it as a sign that my family was healed. A perfect game means so little to anyone who doesn't know baseball and love it like Nicky and Dottie and I did. After those nine other ballpark nights and afternoons, I assigned this perfect game a value it might not deserve. It didn't take me long to wonder if it were true.

I couldn't turn to the numbers I'd penciled so carefully on the Bibb Falk to prove how much it mattered. I could only flash back to the things I saw over the course of nine perfect innings. The things I'd need as a dad every day, some found on the roads that led to the perfect game. Courage and guile and unreasonable devotion. Good fortune, for when I'd feel unsure. Pitching straight on and not around batters, to overcome things that beat me earlier as a dad. Faith and the ability to mount confidence, plus a willingness to ignore trends and imagine better outcomes. And always, setting expectations in place and then releasing them when things get imperfect.

Even though I'd seen that perfect game with my own two eyes, as Dad would say, I craved a screen in those moments. Watching any event was just more real and official if it was on a screen, being narrated by someone. A story told on TV made everything more real in my life. The Rangers' new park had a pristine screen on the Dr. Pepper scoreboard, the one directly opposite our seats. On that screen, the triumphant Rogers grinned for KVTV Channel 11 and answered questions in a halting small town accent.

The noise of the crowd rattled off the skybox fronts. Beside me and waving his Indians cap amid a sea of Rangers fans, Nicky beamed, laughing and hooting. Dot hollered along with us. Then the park got quiet again while the pitcher talked into the camera, his smile growing wider behind a headset, pretty much speechless except for varieties of "I didn't expect this," or "No, I didn't see it coming." Nobody could expect Perfect Game Number 14 in baseball history, because perfect is never expected. My heart buzzed at the luck of finding perfection when I wasn't looking for it.

The voice of the ballpark's announcer rode into the air with a tone as sweet as an aria. "Ladies and gentlemen, a perfect game," the announcer said, "from Kenny Rogers and your Texas Rangers." From the Rangers, indeed. No perfecto is possible without players backing up the pitcher. No sound was richer than the rising chirp of Nicky's voice, captured on my recorder. "We just saw a perfect game," he crowed.

When we finally walked to the exit, I added it up. Of all the games Nicky and I saw on that trip, this was the first one with our family gathered in full. It was a sign of more than what was there. The game was perfect because of what was absent on that night, the hits and walks and errors all removed by skill and by luck at the very last. The elimination of offensive acts shimmered like a guide to making a perfect family. The moment made me savor more of the Almighty's everyday gifts. After that desperate ball caught by a diving rookie, I believed in angels in flight, delivering perfection on a hot summer night.

OUR TRIP'S THIRD AND FINAL FRIDAY DAWNED with the lights of the perfect night still shining. I bolted downstairs to the hotel lobby to snag newspapers, anxious to get copies before they were all snatched up. The *Morning News* and the *Star-Telegram* were ablaze with joy over the perfecto. I could linger over a breakfast buffet with Dottie. By the time we made our way back down to the buffet Nicky was already there, wolfing down an array of pancakes,

French toast, and Belgian waffles.

While breakfast disappeared into him, I pawed through the papers, reading out loud in my ham actor voice. Other diners turned and smiled at it all. I wore my cap festooned with ballpark pins. It was the headgear of a superfan. Other fans asked if we'd been at the game.

"Absolutely," I said. "All three of us were there."

To me, describing the game as a family experience was as important as the miracle we saw. It wouldn't have been perfect without Nicky's stair-mom alongside us; no account I could've given her about the night would've ever matched the joy we had together. Nicky told the story to the other diners as well as I might have, gushing about all the baseball we shared over the past two weeks.

I turned our Sunbird toward Austin and home. I felt inspired that I might turn my life toward hope and natural joy, allowing moments of perfection to come to me unbidden. At each park I'd tried to make the experience perfect, but I couldn't get there on my own.

When the baseball gods delivered that official perfect game to us, I caught a glimpse of the habit I could break: yearning and planning for something better and breathing in anxiety. Insisting everything meet my expectations— and then becoming an insecure father when it did not. The night at a shiny new ballpark proved I might get something better than I could imagine. I had to show up to attract the luck, though. I discovered lucky, the perfect moments in the unplanned joys on our road: following those peaceful Dead Heads, slamming the joysticks of NBA Jam, or tossing a game of catch in an empty parking lot.

During those two weeks I won a glimpse of a gentle and safe life, a time I was caring full-time for my boy, far from the comforts and certainties of home. A vision doesn't complete a picture. We drove thousands of miles to Wrigley and back to experience the majesty of baseball, then found it stamped into history at the Ballpark in Arlington. In the years to come, I'd discover my heart hadn't made it all the way home yet. A boy smaller than Nicky helped me cross the plate.

HOME AT LAST

In baseball, the hardest base to steal is home plate. My next decade after the perfect game was as daunting as the last 90 feet between third and home. I was stuck between those bases in a rundown play, trying to avoid being tagged out. Battles with anxiety, along with my manic moments, continued to pepper my life after the trip.

One score I was able to settle, though, was with my own father. I still had to make my own plays in the field, an outfielder learning to track the flight of the balls hit toward me. I could rescue fatherhood, finding forgiveness as I excused my dad's efforts to father us. I waited a long time for the moment when I'd stop asking why Dad left us. The story had changed.

For years after his suicide, all I could tell anyone was that my father died. I'd say it in a tone that invited no follow-up questions. My ready answer for how he died evolved into "a shooting accident." The next question was always, "How old were you?" I'd round down to make my answer more dramatic, saying, "Only 20." In truth I was five weeks short of my 21st birthday. It was a birthday I'd been anticipating since I left Dad's house. As a soldier I would be a man in his eyes. Dad would have to see me that way. I imagined my birthday as the end of waiting for his praise to surface. It would feel like the encouragement he gave me for my work on our project of paneling that basement. Once he died, I had to build that praise for myself. He might have approved of my initiative.

Even still, each time I get to tell that story now, I'm never certain I've finished searching for answers about his death. It's not as simple as "he was too sad" or "his parents gave him a poor blueprint to build a marriage and family." The reasons resemble the thin, onionskin paper I first learned to touch-type on. The answers are not easily altered—so I try not to erase what I've learned, because the paper will come apart like that onionskin.

He was forced from his job by his health. He didn't have the moxie to start over, or even to recover his pride with the energy I saw in him on the evenings he taught night school at the technical college. He was unsure about his fatherhood from the start. I learned about such things in pieces after he left. After enough years passed, the jigsaw of our lives felt complete.

The perfect game trip started to rescue my memories of Dad. Across dozens of hours at the wheel of the convertible, driving through all of those states, I compared myself to him. I began to jot down the plays where he made his errors. To stay on the winning path, baseball players need backup in the field, one teammate playing behind another to limit the damage of a hit or an error and keep a run off the board. No one could ever back up Dad's play. He wouldn't allow it. Dottie backed up mine until I could learn to pick up the flight of the balls that were hammered toward me in life.

Lots of us have family history to play through. We take our cuts at life's curveballs while we stand at the plate, fouling off pitches to stay alive and avoid going out. A historic baseball game that I was lucky enough to see came with an indelible vision, one that kept me in the game until it generated its backup, too. A new generation of children, starting with Nicky's first, gave me the best sign to steal my way home for good. Perfection can vanish when I seek it through compulsion. But perfect is not a mirage. I can find my moments of oasis.

I SIT ON THE BLEACHER PLANK AND WATCH the little six-year-old on the field. He is small for his age, just like I was and like Nicky was. Noah's white baseball pants crowd the tops of his athletic shoes, while his Astros jersey hangs loose off of his slight shoulders. But my grandson Noah, chip off the old block, holds his chest high as he stands in the on-deck circle. He swings his bat in practice strokes. This is his first T-ball game, the year when nobody plays perfect and everybody is happy. He wears a jersey with only his first name on the back and no hits yet in his short life. I balance a scorebook on my knees, making marks on another set of blue-lined pages with their boxes, and I measure my own progress.

I've sat here before, keeping score in front of a Seybold son. Tonight Noah's daddy shows off the things that I see him passing on to his little boy. Confidence, laughter, and the ease of the certainty that knows the way to happiness. Nicky has grown to become Nick, his chipper chin of an 11-year-old now filled out to a man's jawline in his 30s, his tousled locks now trimmed to a haircut that's as short as a golf course green. He volunteers for Noah's team wearing the garb of success: family. We've travelled far to get here, all of us, to this ballpark debut of the little boy I call Seybold 4.0. I like the sound of that, like a high grade, a fresh place after Dad, me, and then Nick, and finally Noah. Nick now has his dad in the stands while he watches his little boy's debut. Three generations at one ballgame are a first for my family.

Like my dad, Nick has fathered his own two boys, but he is a better dad than me, the fella he has come to call Pop. I like the name, the casual love it carries. Nick's been enriched by fatherhood. He can span the needs of his two boys, youngsters more than three years apart, during those afternoons when he plays with both of them in the back yard. Tonight Nick keeps score for his son's team just as I did—but then he hands his scorebook to me, his sometimes-wild father, so he can coach out on the field. Although I am an older man of more than 60, I am still a young grandfather, new to the part. That's a role Dad never played, taking himself out of the game while still short of this joy.

I've survived beyond the mile-markers of my father's darkest nights. My highs and lows still course through me. I feel the daunting drama of anxiety, the thud in my chest that I detest just like Dad must have. More than fifteen years of therapy and as just many of essential drugs are now the everyday governors on my emotional engine. These help me take the scorebook from Nick with gratitude, a smile, and few worries about being perfect.

I know that mental disorder can never be erased, but I can always get better. Not perfect, not ever. First across those two weeks of that summer, and now through the 25 years beyond, I pursue better. I try not to seek perfect. The moments like this one in the T-ball bleachers, when I find unbidden joy, these will always be my peaks. Valleys of doubt lie all around me. I live in them both because I am a Seybold father—but also one who has stayed in the game to rescue his fatherhood.

Noah takes a swing at the teed-up ball, and with the clank of the bat he runs, fast and short like his grandpa and his father, churning toward a spot of safety on first base. He stands on the bag and beams at the applause and cheers from parents and friends, a group of mothers, fathers, and siblings who I am certain that I belong with. I don't doubt that, not like I did in that Little League springtime with Nicky. Perfection comes delivered by good fortune, not a thing that can be captured by any compulsive plan. I can be secure even though I've had many game days as an unsure father.

Noah is shining in the night's moment, his very first as a bright star in a galaxy of teammates. They back him up. When he steals the next base and the next he runs as part of a team, carrying the desires of his mates. When he stops to stand on each base, beaming at the cheers on his first sports night, it feels different to me while it is brand-new to him. His daddy ran these base paths in Austin where I watched him from a scorer's table, sure of my place there at least. I now look over to my son, who's returned to the game that I loved first as a boy, a game of order and tradition and rituals. I wrote down every play of Nicky's team in his Little League season in the Bibb Falk, trying to use his plays to prove I was a man good enough to be an accomplished dad. As a young father, a man of divorce and then remarriage, I took wild swings. During that summer road trip season with Nicky, I started to lift safer hits into the field of life.

Nobody can foretell the night of a perfect game. Unlike a championship game, it's not a ticket you can buy in advance, no matter how much you spend. Out of more than 210,000 major league games ever played, only 23 have been perfect. Only nine have been achieved since our night in Arlington 25 years ago. Tomorrow, though, could bring another one. Of all the tickets ever sold in major league baseball, buying one to see a perfecto is a 6,400-1 shot when you add it up. Simply luck. My faith in fathering began to shift because of that luck. There are two kinds of luck, though—the kind that finds you, plus the kind you make. I needed both. I had to be on the road for two weeks of ballgames, reaching for love and waiting on its fat pitch, or else that two hours and eight minutes of game time perfection would have eluded me.

Sometimes I believe if Dad had seen that kind of perfection, maybe next to me, he might have survived his sadness. A perfecto might have calmed his obsessive pursuit of perfect, convincing him something better and unexpected could be waiting at the plate. Dad had to keep showing up at the games of life, though. I discovered that if you're at a game together, perfect is where you find it.

There's even more joy if you're seated by First Pitch.

I jot down the start time for Noah's game. The clank of a bat from a teammate lifts my eyes away from the scorebook. Safe at third, Noah is heading for home. My little boy's little boy steals home with joy. I am stealing away from an unsure father's darkness by running toward home, following the light of a son.

ACKNOWLEDGEMENTS

Epic stories cross the plate with a loaded lineup of help. Little of this story would be possible without that first sportswriting job from my editor at the *Hill Country News*, Jim Lindsey. I came to him with no sportswriting experience. He was patient, earnest, and helpful in the way a good father can be for a young man. Jim filled a few of the gaps Dad left behind. Learning to fill a Bibb Falk with ballgame action was a skill I learned in Jim's employ.

While I wrote this, I led memoir workshops with gifted writers in Austin, all of whom helped me stay true to the story. Thanks to Leesa Ross, Kara Bell, Anne Bayerkohler, Dave Barstow, and Melissa Stoeltje, as well as Linda Thune and Mark Stoub and Marie Rivers. Their attention to details, insights, and encouragement gave this book the sweet spot for it to grow up. Many of those writers came into my life through the Writer's League of Texas, where a summertime agents and editors conference gathered us together year after year. I was carried along to finish what I started by kind reading from Donna Johnson. There would be no memoir without my therapist Jim Hoadley.

After mom died, it was time to write about our family. When I was at a loss for a structure for a story told over three decades, author coach Steve Adams gave me a winning game plan. Once I showed up years later with a tangle of ardent work, my editor Dan Crissman laid down the baselines to keep the ball in play. Both were good sports about my writerly foul balls. I got lucky enough to find Asya Blue, whose designs made a classic ballpark of a book where this story could play out.

A fellow has to keep his eye on the ball while writing a story with so many at bats. I give thanks for my brother Bob and sister Tina who prodded me with memories and endured my version of the truth that we all lived through. My beloved Dot helped me remember why I was telling this story—enduring the solitude of my revisions, reading them to make the book shine as bright as my hopes, and always cheering for *Stealing Home* to cross the plate. When it happens with family, it can be perfect.

RESOURCES AND INSPIRATIONS

Perfect: The Inside Story of Baseball's Twenty Perfect Games; James Buckley Jr.

Almost Perfect: The Heartbreaking Pursuit of Baseball's Holy Grail; Joe Cox

Wrigley Field Year by Year: A Century at the Friendly Confines; Joe Pathy

How to Speak Baseball; James Charlton, Sally Cook, and Ross MacDonald

Smart Baseball; Keith Law

Fodor's Ballpark Vacations; Bruce Adams and Margaret Engel

The Joy of Keeping Score; Paul Dickson

The Official Baseball Atlas, 1994 Edition; Rand McNally

The Sporting News Baseball Guide, 1994 Edition

Street and Smith's Baseball 1994

Father's Day; Buzz Bissinger

The Life and Times of the Thunderbolt Kid; Bill Bryson

The Ultimate Baseball Road Trip; A Fan's Guide to Major League Stadiums; Josh Pahigian and Kevin O'Connell

I Don't Care If We Never Get Back: 30 Games in 30 Days on the Best Worst Baseball Road Trip Ever; Ben Blatt and Eric Brewster

Senior Year: A Father, A Son, and High School Baseball; Dan Shaughnessy

A Drive Into the Gap; Kevin Guilfoile

Wishing My Father Well; A Memoir of Fathers, Sons, and Fly-fishing; William Plummer

And of course, Baseball-Reference.com

Follow the author on Goodreads, Amazon, at @ronseybold on Twitter and Instagram, and at ronseybold.com

Stay in the game with the *Stealing Home* baseball newsletter, available at ronseybold.com — keep up with changes in the game, hear stories and bonus material as well as podcasts. Subscribe for giveaways and contest prizes at roadtotheperfectgame.com.

Listen to the author read the *Stealing Home* audiobook from Skin Horse Press, sold at Audible and other audiobook outlets.

www.ingramcontent.com/pod-product-compliance
Lightning Source LLC
Chambersburg PA
CBHW030443300426
44112CB00009B/1136